When Winter Comes

Scripture Reflections for Daily Living

Judy —

God Loves You

Jim Welter

James R. Welter

Foreword by Rev. Msgr. Joseph F. Schaedel
Vicar General, Archdiocese of Indianapolis

ASCENDING
VIEW
PUBLICATIONS

Layout and Cover Design by Mark A. Welter
Cover Photography by Helen F. Welter
Edited by James R. Welter II

ISBN: 1-59352-005-0

Printed in the United States of America
by Christian Services Network
El Cajon, CA

Dedication

This book is dedicated to

My Sister

Frances Welter Avila

1937 – 1995

Fran always believed I could do anything

and to

William Lutton

My Sixth Grade Teacher and Mentor

The First Person Who Encouraged Me to Write

Acknowledgements

No one is quite as amazed at the reality of this book as I am. I have been an accountant all my professional life. Even after returning to college in 1993 to obtain my Religious Studies Degree and entering parish ministry, my duties still included accounting. Perhaps it is my accounting background that yields the gift of getting to the "bottom line" in scripture.

What you read here has, of course, been edited. In some cases it has been extensively edited – one is tempted to say "with a vengeance" – by my sons. It seems that everyone in the family writes better than Dad – yet here I am! It's truly amazing what the Lord can do with an accountant (and two sons with journalism backgrounds)!

To say "I couldn't have done it without them" is a trite – yet true – statement. So I want to acknowledge those who made this book possible:

Helen Fritz Welter, RN, CRNH
Even in the "winters" of our thirty-three years together, Helen still believed I was a poet trapped in an accountant's body. This book is her vindication!

James R. Welter II, MA, University of CT
Our philosopher-son. When he got too old to be sent to his room, I began listening to his ideas. Thanks, Jim, for your suggestions and clarifications during the many hours you spent editing. You made the "old man" look good.

(continued)

Mark A. Welter, BA, Purdue University
Thanks for your many creative layout and design ideas. They make *When Winter Comes* more appealing and readable. Many will select our book because of your efforts.

Patricia A. Ley, MA, LMFT
The skill and dedication you bring to your profession made this book possible. The journey inward is difficult and often painful; an alert reader will see your hand in this work.

The many people who receive my scripture reflections by e-mail and have encouraged me to gather them into this book. As we discern God's calling in life, it is good for us to listen to the voice of others and to follow our gifts. It is the voices of so many of you, and your affirmation of my work, that has brought this vision to life.

Foreword

I consider Jim Welter to be something of a pioneer in his use of the Internet to spread The Word. His vision of bringing scripture readings and prayerful reflection into the workplace and into the home each day has become a nationwide ministry.

I begin each day's meditation with the Lectionary readings and Jim's reflections. In fact, they have been a great help to me in preparing short homilies for daily Mass. I am delighted that Jim has gathered his reflections into this book.

St. John tells us the story of Jesus appearing to the disciples in the Upper Room. Scripture tells us, "Thomas is not with them." When Thomas returns, the other disciples tell him, "We have seen the Lord!" "He has risen!" They are so excited; they want Thomas to believe too. They want Thomas to share in their excitement. They try to give him their faith. But they must learn, as we must learn, that faith cannot be given to anyone – not to our children, not to our spouse, not to our friends.

It doesn't matter how excited we are, or what our faith might mean to us. Each person must come to faith through his or her own experience; all we can do is invite them. And that is what Jesus does when He says, "Come, touch my wounds."

(continued)

Through many stories, anecdotes and observations, Jim relates scripture to everyday life. He shares his good times and his disappointments, his laughter and his tears. These insightful reflections are written with the clarity, sensitivity, and humor born of Jim's life experience as a pastoral minister, public speaker, writer, scholar, and businessman.

Jim's words and the scriptures stay with me as I pray, as I drive to work, while I am facing challenges, making choices, or just *being* with others. As we live our lives in the challenge and comfort of the words of Jesus, our relationship will grow and He will surely sustain us *When Winter Comes.*

In God's never-failing Providence,

Rev. Joseph F. Schaedel

Rev. Msgr. Joseph F. Schaedel
Vicar General and Moderator of the Curia
Archdiocese of Indianapolis

Introduction

This collection of scripture reflections, *When Winter Comes*, began as a ministry to shut-ins. My vision was to use the Internet to reach parishioners who could not attend Mass or parish activities, enabling them to stay connected to the Church. Due to the Pastor's heavy schedule, it was by default that I began writing these reflections on the daily readings. In less than two years, my vision of two hundred subscribers grew to an audience of more than four thousand people across multiple states and around the world. It was in the voices of so many of these people that I felt the prompting of the Spirit to gather my thoughts into this book.

Life was hard on the farm in northern Indiana. We were a family of seven children being raised by a single parent. Like many farm families, much of our time and energy was focused on survival. In summer, life was good – there were always garden vegetables, apples, and other fruits to eat. But we knew that the good time was short, so we spent all summer picking apples, pulling beans, and digging potatoes to prepare for winter.

So it is with our lives. Our time is short. It is important that we too do our "gathering." It is in our good times – our laughing, fun times – that we build our friendships and memories. And it is from these friendships and these memories that we draw our strength when our "winter" comes. *(continued)*

So it is, also, with God's Word. It is my hope that these reflections will draw you into God's Word, and that His Word will become for you a source of strength *"When Winter Comes."*

This book should not be read in one sitting. It is my intention that you spend some quiet time with each reflection. Space has also been provided for recording your thoughts. I invite you to write your own reflections on how each passage speaks to you or applies to your life. I hope, too, that you will re-read this book from time to time. As you grow and have new experiences, new meanings and new insights will emerge from these passages.

The Bible is truly the *living* Word of God.

Peace,

Jim Welter

Table of Contents

The First Chapter:
Come Back to Me

Every temptation is an invitation to "come into my world." Come into my world and accept my values. Come into my world and accept my priorities. Come into my world and accept my lifestyle. Jesus has an invitation for us, too: "Come back to me." Come *back* into my world. Come back, where the yoke is easy and the burden is light. Come back to hope. Come back to love. Come back to healing and forgiveness.

Why do we not run to him? Why do we hesitate? The hymn "Hosea" includes the line "Come back to me with all your heart / don't let fear keep us apart." What do we fear? Punishment? There is no example in scripture of a repentant sinner being punished! We fear *change*. We crave the known. We crave the predictable. We crave the things that are familiar to us: our habits and our demons are familiar companions. We often cling to them, and revel in the illusion of their comfort and security. We dread change as much as we desire the healing that Jesus offers.

What will you ask of me, O Lord? To forgive? To let go? To follow?

The one who holds us so gently now, who gazes at us with such compassion and love, understands our struggles and invites us home.

Come Back To Me   Hosea 2:21

I will espouse you to me forever:
> *I will espouse you in right and in justice,*
> *in love and in mercy;*
I will espouse you in fidelity,
> *and you shall know the LORD.*

Whenever I see a reading from Hosea, a hymn we so often sing during Lent comes to mind. Its haunting refrain – "Come back to me with all your heart / Don't let fear keep us apart" – captures well the theme of the writings of Hosea. Hosea is the prophet of God's love and mercy. He is married to a woman (Gomer) who repeatedly wanders away and is involved in other relationships. Again and again, God calls Hosea to welcome his wife back. This call mirrors God's own actions toward his people, to whom he is wed and has pledged his love. It also mirrors God's call to us.

God always invites us back. He doesn't do this because we have earned it – he invites us back because that's what a loving God does. God remains true to himself. His invitation is not dependent on our response; it is not dependent on anything we might or might not do. If it was dependent on us in any way, we would be in control. We would have power over God!

Relationships run into difficulty when we give power to another person. We give them power over us when we allow them to dictate our actions, as if we had no choices open to us – and no power to choose our response. "She got angry, so I got angry; she yelled, so I yelled. He had an affair, so I had an affair." All of these statements are adult versions of the old "he-hit-me-first" argument (which we do not accept from our children!).

God invites Hosea to be true to himself. God challenges Hosea to welcome his wife back – not because she deserves it, but because Hosea is a good and loving person and that's the kind of thing such people do. Shakespeare said it best: "This above all: to thine own self be true." In being true to our "best self," we invite others to change their behavior and be true to their best selves. We invite them to live out of the "center" of who they are. We invite them to live out of the core of their being.

"To thine own self be true" is God's invitation to us – indeed, it is God's expectation. Matthew (9:20-21) tells the story of a woman who needs healing and follows Jesus. She seeks to "only touch his cloak" – and in so doing, she calls out the best in Jesus! She reaches out and invites Jesus to respond in a certain way: she invites him to heal her, to let her see God in him.

When we live out of our "best self," we let others see God in us as well. It is a loving, forgiving, and healing God that we reveal in those moments – just as Jesus did.

What will you do today, to let others see God in you?

Choosing Judas   Luke 6:12-13

[Jesus] departed to the mountain to pray, and he spent the night in prayer to God. When day came, he called his disciples to himself, and from them he chose twelve, whom he also named apostles.

One of the characteristics of Luke's gospel is his portrayal of Jesus as a man of prayer. Before any major event in Luke's gospel, we encounter Jesus praying. So, before he chooses the Apostles, Luke tells us that "Jesus departed to the mountain to pray..."

I find it interesting that even after praying and asking for guidance, Jesus still chose one who would betray him. Did God "plant" that person to "sabotage" the mission of Jesus or to bring about his death? That would not be an action I would expect from a loving God: "I'll give you eleven good ones – and one that will kill you!" Actually, I suspect the prayer of Jesus centered more on himself. I suspect he prayed that he would be a good leader and would choose those who could best help him fulfill his mission to bring about God's Kingdom. He must have questioned the answer to that prayer many, many times throughout his ministry: "How long must I put up with you?" Or to Peter: "Get behind me, you Satan!" And of course: "One of you will betray me."

No, God didn't have to "plant" a betrayer. Human nature being what it is, Jesus must have known there would be at least one who wouldn't "get it." He must have known there would be at least one who didn't share his vision, at least one with a hidden agenda. There would be at least one whose own baggage, whose own hurts, did not allow him to trust. There would be at least one whose pain did not allow him to believe in friendship, who could not understand how much Jesus cared. There would be at least one who could not allow himself to be vulnerable enough to receive love.

And yet, Jesus felt he had to give even that one a chance... although the final outcome seemed obvious from the start.

Can we do less?

To whom will you give the benefit of the doubt today? To whom will you give a chance... even though he or she may not deserve it?

No Sin Too Great   John 18:26-27

One of the slaves of the high priest, a relative of the one whose ear Peter had cut off, said, "Didn't I see you in the garden with him?" Again Peter denied it. And immediately the cock crowed.

From my office window, I could see the young man knocking on the church door (we keep it locked for security reasons), moving from one door to the next, and looking in the windows. When I let him in, his mood was desperate. "I've got to see a priest!" he said. "It's Monday; the priests have the day off," I replied. "Would you like an appointment?" "No, it can't wait. I need to see one now!" He was almost hyperventilating. "I'm the Pastoral Associate; why don't you and I talk?" I invited him into my office (even as I wondered why these things always seem to happen on Monday!)…

His story was a familiar one: there had been a party with too much drinking, and things had gone way too far. He kept saying, "I can't believe I did that! How could I have done that?" I assured the remorseful young man that God's forgiveness was not dependent upon getting an appointment to see a priest. God forgives at the instant we turn to him.

On the morning following the arrest and trial of Jesus, I think Peter and Judas both must have felt like this young man. "How could I have done that?" they must have asked themselves. The pain we inflict and the evil we are capable of doing often appalls us. Like Peter, we usually don't mean to do it, but fall victim to our weaknesses and fears. To paraphrase St. Paul: "The good that I would, I do not. The evil I would not – that I do!" (Rm 7:19).

So what was the difference between the actions of Peter and Judas? One might be tempted to say that Judas committed the "worse" sin – after all, Judas deliberately betrayed Jesus to those who killed him, while Peter merely denied Jesus in a moment of weakness. The act of Judas was cold and calculated, while Peter's was impulsive, born of weakness and cowardice. But in the end, each denied God!

The difference, then, is that Peter repented and received the forgiveness that was already his for the asking! Even Judas would have received forgiveness, had he repented and turned back to the Lord. Perhaps Judas was too proud to admit his wrongdoing and ask for forgiveness. More likely (since he hanged himself later), he felt that his sin was too serious, too evil, too "big" to be forgiven. After all, he had betrayed the Son of God to his death! Who could ever forgive that?!

God always forgives. Like the Prodigal Son, when we turn homeward… before we even get the words out of our mouth, the ring is back on our finger, the cloak on our shoulders. We have only to repent and turn back to God.

What keeps you from turning homeward today, and trusting in God's forgiveness?

The BE-Attitudes   Matthew 5:1-3

When he saw the crowds, he went up the mountain, and after he had sat down, his disciples came to him. He began to teach them, saying:
> *"Blessed are the poor in spirit,*
> *for theirs is the kingdom of heaven."*

The Beatitudes are found in Matthew's gospel (the Sermon on the Mount), as well as in Luke's gospel (the Sermon on the Plain). A comparison of these versions demonstrates how the gospel writers adapted the teachings of Jesus to their audience and to the problems they were facing.

Matthew portrays Jesus as the "new Moses" in his gospel, so he has Jesus speak from the mountain, which was considered a seat of authority in Biblical times. Matthew's audience was not financially poor, so his gospel uses the term "the poor in spirit." Luke, on the other hand, was speaking to those who were literally sick and poor (and who probably couldn't have climbed a mountain), so he has Jesus saying "blessed are you who are poor." (Luke 6:20)

Many commentators on these passages adopt the phrase "the BE-Attitudes." These attitudes represent what we are to BE as Christians: meek, merciful, thirsting for holiness, and comforting to those who mourn.

But on another level, we are asked to adopt an attitude of "BE-ing." Our culture would have us believe that we must "do" something in order to have value – we must "achieve" and "produce." But, as my wife is fond of reminding me, we are human "be-ings," not human "do-ings"! This passage reminds us that our true value is in "be-ing" – being merciful, being kind, being meek. We are to "be" with each other in sorrow. We are to "be" there to show mercy. We are to "be" there when others are hungry, thirsty, or in need. We are to "be" there to comfort, to listen, and to love.

Christian life is also "BE-ing" together. What if we looked at everyone else as "one of us"? What if we erased the dividing lines, and discarded the divisive groupings of "us" and "them"? What if we embraced oneness, and the art of "BE-ing" together? Would it change our attitudes? "One of us" will be executed today. "One of us" got drunk and drove a car that hit another "one of us." A terrorist becomes "one of us," and his victim is also "one of us."

Can we open our hearts and "be" together today? Can we "be" with those we love, and with those we don't? Can we "be" with those we trust, and also "be" with those who frighten us? Can we "be" with those who have helped, and with those who have injured us? Can we "be" with those who forgive us, and with those who don't?

Who will you "be" with today?

The Unforgivable Sin   Mark 3:28-29

"Amen, I say to you, all sins and all blasphemies that people utter will be forgiven them. But whoever blasphemes against the Holy Spirit will never have forgiveness, but is guilty of an everlasting sin."

This reading sometimes troubles people, because Jesus talks about the "unforgivable sin." They wonder what this sin could be, and fear they may have committed it. The existence of an "unforgivable" sin also presents the possibility that we can do something God will not forgive.

We have been taught that God is all-powerful and can do anything. This statement never fails to prompt the Theology 101 question: "Can God make a rock that he can't lift?" We sometimes forget that there are things God cannot do! God cannot do things that are logically self-contradictory (like making a square circle, or a rock that he can't lift). God cannot do those things that go against his nature: God cannot stop loving and God cannot hate (because God is Love). And God cannot forgive when there is no repentance.

Is there really a sin that God will not forgive? I think what we have here is the same "limit" on forgiveness that we allude to in the Lord's Prayer: "Forgive us our trespasses, as we forgive those who trespass against us…" We are not asking God to keep score in this prayer, or to play a game of "tit for tat" with us. Rather, we are acknowledging that God can only forgive us to the extent that we are open to receiving forgiveness. The act that opens us to receiving forgiveness is our willingness to forgive others. That line in the Lord's Prayer is not a negative thing: we pray for all the forgiveness that we are capable of receiving, and God gives us all the forgiveness that we can accept.

It isn't that God "will not" forgive us in certain instances – rather, in a sense, he *cannot* forgive us, because we will not accept his forgiveness. If we refuse to forgive others, we are refusing to open our hearts to God's mercy – and so we reject God's Holy Spirit and our sin becomes "unforgivable."   But, if we turn to God in sincere repentance and express that attitude by forgiving others, then there is no wrongdoing God cannot pardon, and no sin from which he will not set us free.

Who must you forgive today, to open yourself to the fullness and forgiveness of Christ?

Moving the Fence   Matthew 23:16-19

"Woe to you, blind guides, who say, 'If one swears by the temple, it means nothing, but if one swears by the gold of the temple, one is obligated.' Blind fools, which is greater, the gold, or the temple that made the gold sacred? And you say, 'If one swears by the altar, it means nothing, but if one swears by the gift on the altar, one is obligated.' You blind ones, which is greater, the gift, or the altar that makes the gift sacred?"

One of the most beautiful images in scripture is Jacob's dream of the ladder (or stairway) to heaven. In that story, God opened a door for Jacob that brought him and his people into a new relationship. In the above gospel story, Jesus stuns the local religious leaders by asserting that they have closed that door not only for themselves, but for others as well. The word "woe" is also translated as "alas," it is as much an expression of sorrowful pity as it is of anger. Jesus was angry and disappointed with the religious leaders because they had failed to listen to God's word and had misled the people they were supposed to guide. "Blind guides," you don't understand what's important – you yourselves miss the point, so how can you lead others? Jesus then gives a series of examples to show how they themselves were misguided. In their zeal to win converts, they required unnecessary and burdensome rules which obscured the more important aspects of religion, such as love of God and love of neighbor. They were leading people to legalism, rather than to God.

When Winter Comes   James R. Welter

How often we too close the door to God, for ourselves and for others, by insisting on "the rules" – as if God, who created the universe, can't operate outside the box *we* have drawn! Legalism looks for ways to exclude people, ways to close the door. God finds ways to include us; he keeps the door open.

In pre-Vatican II days, there were restrictions about who could be buried in a Catholic cemetery. Public sinners, those married outside the church, etc., were excluded. Most cemeteries had some type of fence around them, so reference was made to those who were "buried outside the fence." There was a story about a Pastor who was deeply troubled by this law, which required someone he knew to be buried "outside the fence." Finally, he could stand it no longer. So, in the middle of the night he got up, went to the cemetery, and moved the fence so that it included the person who was excluded by "the law."

That's what God does... he moves the fence for us!

Unclean Spirits — Mark 1:23-24

In their synagogue was a man with an unclean spirit; he cried out, "What have you to do with us, Jesus of Nazareth? Have you come to destroy us?"

A man with an unclean spirit comes into the synagogue where Jesus is teaching. Immediately, the unclean spirit is afraid and screeches at Jesus, "What do you want of us? Have you come to destroy us?"

I often tell people that, if the gospel leaves you feeling too comfortable, maybe you need to read it again! The first time I read this gospel story, it was easy: I pictured myself as one of the bystanders in the synagogue, amazed as the scene unfolded. And then I read it again. This time, I am not a bystander... *I* am the one with the unclean spirit.

Unclean? How often do we stop to realize that our lives are messy and less-than-perfect? Our failed attempts to be kind or honest, our motives that are less than pure, and our struggles to control our appetites, desires, and addictions are all areas that need healing. We, too, are "unclean."

And so we enter the synagogue with our "unclean spirits" and encounter Jesus teaching. The unclean part of us recoils with fear and dread: what will Jesus want of us? Will he destroy us? No – he heals us. With great conviction and authority, Jesus addresses the screeching of our "unclean spirits" and sends them out of us. But it isn't something that happens easily: the man in the gospel has a violent convulsion and makes a loud shrieking as the spirit leaves him. Aren't we often like that, too? No matter how much we want to change and rid ourselves of our "unclean spirits," we instead cling to them – to our habits – as familiar companions. We dread the change that Jesus will cause as much as we desire his healing.

The one who holds us so gently now, who gazes at us with such compassion and love, understands our struggles and knows that letting go of our "unclean spirits" is a lifetime process.

Jesus has touched us… our healing has just begun.

~ Your Reflection ~

Weeds and Wheat   Matthew 13:27-29

The slaves of the householder came to him and said, "Master, did you not sow good seed in your field? Where have the weeds come from?" He answered, "An enemy has done this." His slaves said to him, "Do you want us to go and pull them up?" He replied, "No, if you pull up the weeds you might uproot the wheat along with them."

When I was growing up on the farm, the garden was a major source of food for our family. We were a family of seven being raised by a single mother. Money was very tight; the garden was the best way to stretch a dollar. We grew a lot of beans, and we pulled a lot of weeds. As children, it wasn't always clear to us what was a plant and what was a weed, and we would get in lots of trouble if we pulled up the plants. So, when in doubt, I would call my older sister Fran over and ask her, "Is this a plant or a weed?" Fran always knew. Sometimes she would say that it was a weed, but that I should leave it alone: "It's too close to the plant; if you pull the weed, you'll kill the plant."

This parable from Matthew is about judgment. It cautions us not to judge before "the play is done," before "the fat lady sings," before the harvest comes. In the meantime, "the rain falls on the just and the unjust alike." The weeds and the wheat grow side by side; they are all part of the field, and to root out the weeds at this stage would destroy the wheat along with them. We must have patience. We must wait for the harvest.

On another level, I think we are also being called to an acceptance of our own humanness. In every heart, there are weeds and wheat, good and evil, light and shadow. *Make Friends With Your Shadow* was a popular spiritual book a decade or so ago. In it, the author suggested that we shouldn't strive to "root out" or deny our "shadow" side, but instead "make friends" with it. That is, recognize it, name it, and accept it as part of us, part of the "field" of our being. All the various "twelve-step" programs also recognize this need.

I've always been a control freak; it's my "original sin." If, by some miracle, I could "root" that out of my personality, I would no longer be *me* – and all that is good and worthwhile about being "me" would also perish. Pulling the "weed" would destroy the "wheat"! So I must learn to accept the "weeds" in me – but, it is said, "If you can name it, you can tame it!" So, by recognizing my faults, flaws, and shortcomings, I can (with God's help) tame and harness them. I may even be able to turn them to a good purpose ("control freaks" make great administrators, business managers, and accountants!). Maybe that's why God allows such "burdens" to remain in our lives – so that, as we strive to overcome them, we become stronger, more loving people.

This, then, is our challenge and our struggle; our goal and our goodness; our cross and our crown.

Fran has been gone for more than six years now. I miss her today. As I look at my life, I want to call her over one more time and ask, "Is this a plant or a weed?"

The Second Chapter:
God's Loving Care

I was 29 years old before I began to suspect that God loved me. I was 35 years old before I was convinced of it!

The image of God's loving care does not come easily for me. Ours was not an emotionally expressive family; I was 40 years old before I told my mother that I loved her. My father died without ever hearing those words from me. I was raised in the black-and-white world of the Baltimore Catechism: my God was a legalistic God. My God was a policeman in the sky, an accountant God who kept track of everything I did. Although I have come to know God's love through the love of my wife and children, I still struggle with the image of living in God's loving care.

To experience God's loving care, Jesus invites us to come as a child. "When you welcome a child, you welcome me." To welcome Jesus and to be one with him, I must welcome the child in *me*. Welcoming the child in me means giving up control and being open to new things. It means acknowledging my hurts and being able to cry. It means being open and honest in my relationships. It means trusting love, and allowing myself to be vulnerable. It means being able to ask forgiveness and say "I'm sorry." It means living in the care of one whose love can "make it all better."

When I welcome the child in me, I make room for Jesus.

19

Feel The Rain   Matthew 5:45-46

"...he makes his sun rise on the bad and the good, and causes rain to fall on the just and the unjust. For if you love those who love you, what recompense will you have? Do not the tax collectors do the same?"

A common phrase being used in reference to our Catholic Church leaders these days is, "They don't get it." So it is with God's love: we just "don't get it." In fact, we have never "gotten it"! "Lord, whose sin caused this man to be blind?" "You're going to throw a party for that runaway son of yours?" "But we worked all day in the sun, and you're paying us the same amount? You're treating them the same as us!"

We just "don't get it"!

This passage from Matthew says, "He causes rain to fall on the just and the unjust." God is good to the unjust as well as the just; God's love embraces saint and sinner alike.

I just don't like to hear that! You mean God loves Osama bin Laden as much as he loves me? That's not fair! I stayed home and worked the farm. I go to Church every Sunday; I take care of my family. I do volunteer work and write scripture reflections three times a week! And God treats one of "them" the same as me?! And what's wrong with the way I love? It seems fair to me – I love my wife, I love my children, I love my family and friends. I love all those who love me!

But that's too easy, Jesus says – anybody can do that. Even tax collectors do that. Even sinners do that. Even Osama bin Laden does that!

If it's deserved, it's not mercy. If it's earned, it's not grace. If it's easy, it's not true love. So you must be more: you must "be perfect, even as your heavenly Father is perfect." You must love as God does – unconditionally. You must let your love fall like the rain, "on the just and the unjust." Let it fall without judgment. Let it fall on those who love you; let it fall on those who hate you. Let it be absorbed by all who feel it.

"Why?" I say. "That doesn't make any sense! Why should I do that?"

"Because God first loved you." Because he loves you now.

Let me feel your love, Lord… falling as soft rain upon my face.

Ninety and Nine   Luke 15:4-6

"What man among you having a hundred sheep and losing one of them would not leave the ninety-nine in the desert and go after the lost one until he finds it? And when he does find it, he sets it on his shoulders with great joy and, upon his arrival home, he calls together his friends and neighbors and says to them, 'Rejoice with me because I have found my lost sheep.'"

As a 52-year-old college freshman, I noticed that the "mature" students were always last to finish the tests. My psychology professor assured me, "It's not because you're slow; it's because you have more information and experience through which to process the questions. Basically, all the traditional students know is what they have learned in class."

I thought of this recently when a "younger" person remarked how difficult it must be to write three scripture reflections a week. But it's not so difficult. Maturity brings with it so much experience to relate to the gospels, and to assess how the Lord has been active in one's life.

That younger person probably doesn't even know about the old comedy team of Abbott and Costello! In a classic routine, Costello (the funny one) sees an attractive woman and says, "She looks like a million bucks!" Abbott (the straight man) replies, "How do you know? You've never seen a million bucks before!" Costello replies, "That's what I mean – she's like something I've never seen before!"

When Winter Comes
James R. Welter

In this passage from Luke, Jesus leaves the ninety-nine sheep and goes in search of the one that is lost. And he calls himself the "Good Shepherd"! For a shepherd who is any good at his job, this makes no sense! He leaves the rest of the flock unattended, at risk, exposed to the wolves, and goes off looking for the one who didn't follow the rules and wandered away?! The "Good" Shepherd? I don't think so! I've never seen a shepherd like that before!

And Jesus says: "That's what I mean – I'm like something you've never seen before!"

Jesus loves us beyond reason. Jesus loves us in spite of what others may think. Jesus loves us even when we wander off, even when we become tangled in the brush of our own bad choices. He seeks us when we are lost, as if we were the only one in the world. And when he finds us, he doesn't get angry or scold us – he rejoices!

He's like something you've never seen before!

Praise him today. Praise him!

Broken Glass Shining   Acts 8:4-8

Now those who had been scattered went about preaching the word. Thus Philip went down to [the] city of Samaria and proclaimed the Messiah to them. With one accord, the crowds paid attention to what was said by Philip when they heard it and saw the signs he was doing. For unclean spirits, crying out in a loud voice, came out of many possessed people, and many paralyzed and crippled people were cured. There was great joy in that city.

There is a page in my copy of Henri Nouwen's book *Life of the Beloved* that is dog-eared, soiled, and worn. It bears the marks of countless hours of prayer and meditation. On that page, Nouwen recalls a scene from Leonard Bernstein's musical "Mass" (written in memory of President Kennedy). A priest, richly dressed in liturgical vestments, is lifted up by his people. He towers high above the adoring crowd, carrying a glass chalice. When the human pyramid collapses, the priest falls to the ground and the chalice is shattered. In the next scene, the priest is in a T-shirt and jeans, walking through the debris of his former glory. He gazes on the broken chalice and mutters, "I never knew... broken glass... could shine so brightly."

It is April 1993. We have two kids in college. The job I loved is gone, a casualty of misunderstanding, betrayal, and falsehood. I was "asked to resign." (That's the politically correct way of saying it; the phrase doesn't make what happened hurt any less.) I'm not a provider anymore. My life is out of control. What happens now?

When Winter Comes   James R. Welter

The gospel tells us again and again not to worry about what "we" can accomplish. We are simply to "believe," and God will take care of "accomplishing things." In scripture, we get a glimpse of how God gets things done even in our adversity. We see it in this passage from Acts – the new Christians were facing persecution and death. People were running for their lives, "scattering throughout the countryside." But even in that scattering, the gospel was spread, as "those who had been scattered went about preaching the word."

As I remember 1993, I marvel at how God manages to get things accomplished. After losing my job, I went back to school and had the privilege of being in college at the same time as my two sons. It's a blessing afforded a very few, and is a highlight of my life. And my Religious Studies degree led to my going to work in the Church. Most days it's an exciting and rewarding second career – new doors have been opened, with possibilities beyond my imagination.

We are broken, Nouwen reminds us. Broken that we might be blessed (by becoming more sensitive, more open, more fully human). And blessed that we might be given (multiplied and used by God to bring about his kingdom).

We don't have to "accomplish" anything, Jesus tells us. All we have to do is believe. Believe that we are clay in God's hands. We are broken pots, repaired and renewed by the Potter.

Broken glass, shining brightly.

I Will Be With You   Exodus 3:10-13

"Come, now! I will send you to Pharaoh to lead my people, the Israelites, out of Egypt." But Moses said to God, "Who am I that I should go to Pharaoh and lead the Israelites out of Egypt?" He answered, "I will be with you; and this shall be your proof that it is I who have sent you: when you bring my people out of Egypt, you will worship God on this very mountain." "But," said Moses to God, "when I go to the Israelites and say to them, 'The God of your fathers has sent me to you,' if they ask me, 'What is his name?' what am I to tell them?"

Moses prays the way I often pray: "Don't send me – send my brother instead! He speaks better than I do; he's taller, younger, stronger, and people like him. He's a natural! If I go, who's going to count the sheep? Who's going to reconcile the bank statements? And my socks! I really have to rearrange my sock drawer. Why me? I don't want to go! Who am I? What will I say? I don't even know your name! How am I going to do this?"

And God answered, "I will be with you."

It is a Saturday morning, in April 1993. I'm alone in the office. The one with a view of downtown. The one with my name on the door. The one I had worked so hard for; the one that signified success and prosperity. My resignation has been accepted. My application for college is in process. I'm back at the office, cleaning out my desk. Suddenly the enormity of the change in my life strikes me:

When Winter Comes

James R. Welter

I haven't been without a job since I was sixteen years old! It's how I provide for my family; it makes me feel secure. It's how I get my identity. It defines me. It's who I am.

Lord! I slump back in my chair. Tears come. "How am I going to do this?"

The next thing I pull out of my desk is a poster. A poster my son had designed years ago for our parish mission. In bold letters is the mission's theme: "I WILL BE WITH YOU."

The bush is still burning. God still talks to his people.

And his message is still the same: "I will be with you... always."

The Shepherd   John 10:2-4

"Whoever enters through the gate is the shepherd of the sheep. The gatekeeper opens it for him, and the sheep hear his voice, as he calls his own sheep by name and leads them out. When he has driven out all his own, he walks ahead of them, and the sheep follow him, because they recognize his voice."

The image of shepherds and sheep is used many times in scripture. I was raised on a farm, and I know that being referred to as a "sheep" isn't very flattering! As kids on the farm, we would make fun of how dumb the sheep were (as compared to our smart cows!). The sheep would eat the grass so close to the root that it wouldn't grow back for a second feeding later that season. If a sheep gets onto its back, it can't get up by itself; it will die if someone doesn't help it get back up. (That's one use of the hook that a shepherd has on the end of his staff… now aren't you glad you read this today?!) And a sheep will literally walk over the edge of a cliff, following its leader. Not exactly the brightest creatures in the animal kingdom!

But while it may not be flattering to be compared to such an animal, the image of sheep and shepherding can teach us much about our relationship with God. At the end of each day, the shepherd brings his sheep into shelter; the sheep know the voice of their shepherd and come at his beckoning. So familiar was the shepherd with his sheep that he called each of them by a distinct name. In Biblical times, sheep were usually kept out in the fields and then gathered into a fold at darkness. The fold was then guarded

29

by a shepherd throughout the night. The shepherd was literally the "door" through which the sheep had to pass to enter the fold. And so the scriptures describe God as a shepherd who brings security and peace to his people: "The LORD will guard your coming and going both now and forever." (Psalm 121:8)

So, Lord, forgive me for wanting to be the *shepherd* instead of one of the sheep. For wanting not only to control *my* life, but the lives of others as well. Forgive me for not walking to the cliff's edge, for fear of what you might ask of me. Help me to follow you, for you know me… and have called me by name.

~ Your Reflection ~

Welcome The Child   Mark 9:36-37

Taking a child he placed it in their midst, and putting his arms around it he said to them, "Whoever receives one child such as this in my name, receives me; and whoever receives me, receives not me but the One who sent me."

This passage is sometimes translated, "Whoever welcomes a child for my sake, welcomes me." Our boys are now both young adults; the hindsight of thirty years gives some insight into the ramifications of the commitment made when a couple "welcomes a child" into their relationship. The mother experiences this first, as her own body changes to "make room" for the child. But Dad soon joins in the worry and loss of sleep that continue through the teenage and college years, and beyond... way, way beyond!

How, in this welcoming of a child, do we welcome Jesus? From the moment of conception, welcoming a child means not living for oneself. It means learning to be "the servant of all." It means being open, listening, and putting the needs of others before my own. At a deeper level, I cannot welcome Jesus until I welcome the child... in me.

It's 1970. Newspapers report the story. A child stands trapped in the fourth-story window of a burning building. The thick, black smoke hides the scene below from view. The fire trucks will not arrive in time. The situation is desperate. "Jump!" he hears his father's voice calling. "I'll catch you!" The boy lets go of the ledge, falls through the darkness – and lands safely in his father's arms.

When Winter Comes

James R. Welter

We do not like the role of "child." We do not "welcome" situations over which we have no control. "Welcoming the child in me" means letting go. It means being open to new things. It means acknowledging my hurts, and being able to cry. It means being open and honest in my relationships. It means trusting love, and allowing myself to be vulnerable. It means saying "I'm sorry," and asking forgiveness. It means believing that there is one whose love can "make it all better," and living in his care.

When I welcome the child in me, I make room for Jesus. Then I can let go of those things to which I cling. Then I can I let go of the ledge. Then I can fall through the darkness...

...knowing that I will land safely in my Father's arms.

Become Like a Child   Matthew 18:2-3

He called a child over, placed it in their midst, and said, "Amen, I say to you, unless you turn and become like children, you will not enter the kingdom of heaven."

It's summer, a lazy Sunday afternoon. The sunlight glistens on the water as the waves gently wash to shore. The beach stretches as far as the eye can see. A child plays in the sand. He builds a castle, and then another. As the sun moves slowly across the sky, a moat emerges and water is brought from the sea in a hundred trips.

Now the sun is low, and the waves increase. "Time to go!" calls a voice from the shore.

The child laughs, watching as everything he has built is washed away. He knows he can't take his castles with him. The joy is in the building. The music is in the song that is sung. The goal is the journey. All is washed back to the sea. It is as it should be.

The day has ended. The child laughs with glee, takes his father's hand, and goes home.

"Unless you become as a little child," Jesus says, "you cannot enter the kingdom."

Throughout our lives we build our castles, toil in the sun, make a hundred trips to the sea. "Time to go!" calls a voice from the shore. The day has ended.

When Winter Comes
James R. Welter

May we, too, know that we can't take our castles with us. The joy is in the building. The music is in the song that is sung. The goal is the journey. All is washed back to the sea.

It is as it should be.

When we hear that voice, may we laugh with glee, take our Father's hand... and go home.

~ Your Reflection ~

Snow Is Falling Somewhere   John 1:4-8

Whoever is without love does not know God, for God is love.

I don't know the name of the song, but I think of it every time the snow falls. The singer compares the love of Jesus to the falling snow. The snow falls on everything, the just and the unjust, the rich and the poor; it covers our failures, our imperfections, and our sinfulness. And "snow is falling somewhere, like the love of Jesus." It's the only line I remember. It's the only line I need.

It is snowing in Indiana, our first of the season, as I write this. I'm enjoying it. I'm delaying going to Mass so I don't have to go out in it, and ignoring the fact that, before the end of the day, I'll be shoveling it from our steps. I am choosing instead to pray with it, to listen to its silence and marvel at its beauty. To let it return me to my childhood on the farm.

Our children are young adults; I'm not going to get away with making snow cream today. Maybe I can manage chili for lunch, though. We always had chili on the cold, snowy days. Maybe I can huddle with my sister Fran again, share our hopes for the future, and make pictures in the frost on the window.

Fran has been gone almost seven years now. I feel her presence today.

"Snow is falling somewhere…"

I love you, Frannie.

When Winter Comes James R. Welter

~ Your Reflection ~

The Third Chapter:
Accepting Jesus

"**J**esus Is The Answer!" We have seen that phrase on bumper stickers and billboards across the country. It reminds us that Jesus is always there for us. He welcomes us in our pain, our wants, and our needs. In these times, we feel his arms around us. His tender gaze warms our being; his words comfort us.

Jesus Is The Question? When things are well with us, Jesus becomes our question and our challenge. What will you do about Jesus? Will you accept him or reject him? "Do not think that I have come to bring peace upon the earth. I have come to bring not peace but the sword." Jesus calls for a decision. Accepting Jesus means accepting both his comfort and his challenge.

So what will You Do? What will you do with this rebel who does things that aren't "religious"? This one who heals on the Sabbath! This one who works when he should be resting; who disobeys the law! What will you do with this one who eats with sinners and heals lepers? What will you do with this one who comes with a sword?

What will you do about Jesus?

Woe To You   Matthew 11:21

"Woe to you, Chorazin! Woe to you, Bethsaida! … But I tell you, it will be more tolerable for the land of Sodom on the day of judgment than for you."

My office phone rang. It was Monday, 8:04 a.m. I had worked for this particular company for fifteen years, to the day. I moved toward my boss' office, anticipating how the occasion would be recognized. Would I receive a bonus? Maybe I'd receive a plaque or a lapel pin? Or perhaps just a handshake and a heartfelt, "thank you for your many years of service…" Instead, without even inviting me to sit down, he said, "We've decided to let you go. Turn in your keys, and be out of here today." More hurtful than the event itself was the fact that they chose to discharge me on my anniversary with the company. Was this an attempt to save the cost of my becoming fully vested in the retirement program? Even more hurtful, though, was the thought that they didn't even realize it was my anniversary. They didn't remember that I was one of the their first employees. It felt like my contributions didn't matter – it was like I had never been there. I was unimportant, a non-entity. The phone rang. My boss turned, indifferent to my presence: "Hello Charlie, about that deal…"

I think I understand how Jesus is feeling in this passage from Matthew. He is being treated with indifference: he feels like he doesn't matter, as though what he says and does is of no importance. He stands in the village square.

When Winter Comes

James R. Welter

These are his people – they have seen him heal the sick, they have heard him cast out demons, they have witnessed his miracles... yet they turn away. They are indifferent to the presence of God in their midst.

When Jesus visited his hometown of Nazareth, he was chased out of town. He was sharply opposed in Jerusalem. But at least, in those places, they recognized him! At least they acknowledged his presence and reacted with some feeling, some passion. At least they had the decency to stone him! But "woe to you," Chorazin and Bethsaida, "for if the mighty deeds done in your midst had been done in Sodom, it would have remained until this day." But you ignore me! I speak, but you do not hear. I heal, but you do not see. You are unaware that I am even here.

"Woe to you," Chorazin and Bethsaida! Had Sodom seen what you have seen, they would have repented and been standing today!

Are we indifferent to God in our midst? Do we say he is first in our life, but complain if Mass takes ten minutes more than we have allotted? Do we treat with indifference that boring person who just wants someone to listen? Do we refuse to see Christ in the toothless woman, who has her story too? Do we walk past Lazarus, begging at our gate? Do we buy him off with the flip of a coin and not look into his eyes?

What will you do today, to show the Lord that you recognize him?

Jesus Is The Question   Matthew 10:34

Do not think that I have come to bring peace upon the earth. I have come to bring not peace but the sword.

It's 1974. We are driving north. Our '71 Chevy is loaded with all the provisions of a young family going to Grandma's. As we pass through the small town of Kokomo, Indiana, our four-year-old son breaks the silence: "Jesus is the answer," he proclaims, with an authority that would make any Chicago street preacher proud. "What did you say?" my wife and I respond in unison. "That sign over there says 'Jesus is the answer,'" comes the reply. (We didn't even know the kid could read!) A pregnant pause… "So… what's the question, Daddy?"

The Spirit was alive and well and visiting Kokomo, Indiana, that day.

"Jesus is the question, son," I replied. "Everyone has to decide what they are going to do about Jesus. Are they with him or against him?"

"You think I have come to bring peace?" Jesus asks in this passage. "Do not think that I have come to bring peace upon the earth. I have come to bring not peace but the sword."

In other words: I didn't come for your entertainment. I didn't come to give you feel-good, bumper-sticker religion. I came to call you to a decision!

When Winter Comes

So you have to make a decision: what will you do with this Rabbi who is doing things that aren't "religious"? This one who heals on the Sabbath! This one who works when he should be resting; who disobeys the law! What will you do with this one who eats with sinners and heals lepers – this one who talks to women, and other "undesirables"?

Make a decision: what will you do with this one who comes with a sword? What will you do about Jesus? Will you look at things in a new way, and allow your beliefs to be   challenged? Are you willing to take a chance? Are you willing to leave your "comfort zone"? Are you willing to do something radical, something that may get you in trouble, laughed at, or condemned?

Jesus calls us to a decision today. He challenges us to look inward. He invites us to go where we have not gone before. He invites us to intimacy ("into-me-I-see"); he invites us to see ourselves as God sees us. He challenges us to make radical decisions – to let go of our possessions. He tells us to love our neighbor… and then he tells us that *everyone* is our neighbor!

Jesus is the answer. But even more – Jesus is the question!

What is *your* answer?

The Hour Of Decision   Acts 12:24-25

But the word of God continued to spread and grow. After Barnabas and Saul completed their relief mission, they returned to Jerusalem, taking with them John, who is called Mark.

It wasn't unusual for me to get a book from my philosopher son for my birthday. But the author he chose prompted a phone call: "Billy Graham?" I asked incredulously. "He doesn't even consider *himself* a deep thinker!" "There's something to be said for consistency," was the response. We had attended a Graham revival just a few years ago. It was bittersweet; Graham was in the winter of his ministry. I remembered the beginning: I was in the fifth grade when I first heard the "Hour of Decision" on the radio.

I have never been very comfortable with the theology that everything comes down to one moment, one time of decision. I am not diminishing the good that Graham has done or calling into question the experience of so many people; I can even point to a moment in my own life after which nothing was the same again. But, with that said, it is my experience that we make *many* "decisions for Christ." Each day, in fact, we are called to say "yes" to Jesus. The above passage from Acts evokes an image of making a decision for Christ, an image of saying, "yes" to Jesus: Barnabas and Saul make a decision to go forth to proclaim the Good News.

When Winter Comes   James R. Welter

For most of us, our "hour of decision" to love and serve the Lord is not a dramatic one. There is no thunderbolt to knock us from our horse; no burning bush. Our "yes" may be simply to respond to the duty of the moment. Our call may be as common as a child's cry at night, or the buzz of an alarm clock in the morning. And in the thousand ways we say "yes," in those thousand everyday decisions to love and serve, we make our "decision" for Christ.

For more than fifty years, Billy Graham has reminded us that salvation is a free gift from God. We do not earn it; we *cannot* earn it. It is already ours. All we have to do is accept it. All we have to do is make a decision for Christ; all we have to do is say "yes" to Jesus. And how do we do that? Matthew reminds us that the only question we will be asked when we stand before the Lord is, "How did you treat the least of my people?" How did you love? How did you serve?

Loving and serving has many dimensions: "confessing" Jesus, yes – in many ways, by word and action; by being baptized (if I'm aware of the ritual and it has meaning to me); by living my Christianity through the denomination that I feel brings me closest to the Lord. But most of all, we say "yes" to Jesus by responding in love each time God's "alarm" sounds.

How will you respond to God's "alarm" today?

The Treasure   Matthew 13:44-46

"The kingdom of heaven is like a treasure buried in a field, which a person finds and hides again, and out of joy goes and sells all that he has and buys that field. Again, the kingdom of heaven is like a merchant searching for fine pearls. When he finds a pearl of great price, he goes and sells all that he has and buys it."

This passage may strike us as a little strange: a man finds a "treasure" (the term is used in general sense – it could mean any item of great value) in a field. He buries it there, and then sells everything he has to buy the field. My accountant's mentality kicks in here: why didn't he just slip the thing in his pocket? Then he would have the treasure and his money as well!

There were no banks or safety-deposit boxes in the time of Jesus, so people often buried their treasures in the ground for safekeeping. And, as is the case even today, whoever owned a piece of land also owned whatever was buried on it. Notice that the man buys the land, not the treasure. Why? The treasure is too valuable – he can't afford to buy it directly, but if he sells everything he has, he will be able to buy the land and thereby possess the treasure. Merely slipping the treasurel in his pocket would not give him legitimate ownership; it would only make him a thief. No, to truly own the treasure, he must let go of everything else and literally "buy the farm."

When Winter Comes James R. Welter

Our life in Christ is priceless! We can't buy it, nor can we obtain it through some easy, undemanding means. We can only obtain that treasure – that life – by letting go of everything else. That's the cost of spiritual freedom. But we often fear to purchase that land, to enter into that relationship with God. Like the ancient Israelites, we prefer to admire the "promised land" from a distance. Real intimacy with God, such as Moses and Jesus experienced, can be frightening! Conversation with God can be intimidating; walking in God's presence can make us tremble. Why? It's not because of anything about God! God loves us and wants what is best for us; his presence is infinitely desirable and precious. The problem is ours! We fear the cost of possession – we are afraid of what we might have to do or change, what we will have to give up, or what may be asked of us. So we look for the easy way out – some way that will not cost so much, that will not call for our total commitment. Some way that will make the burden lighter. Some way to just "slip it in our pocket."

But in doing this, we are kidding ourselves. We know the cost. We have seen it on Calvary.

And yet, as with the man who sold everything he had and bought the field, the treasure – the pearl, the reward – is ultimately worth its price.

What must you "sell" in order to possess it?

Brothers and Sisters of Jesus   Mark 3:31-35

His mother and his brothers arrived. Standing outside they sent word to him and called him. A crowd seated around him told him, "Your mother and your brothers [and your sisters] are outside asking for you." But he said to them in reply, "Who are my mother and [my] brothers?" And looking around at those seated in the circle he said, "Here are my mother and my brothers. [For] whoever does the will of God is my brother and sister and mother."

In this passage, we get a glimpse of a very human event in the life of Jesus. His family arrives in the town where he is teaching. They have heard stories and seem to think he is a little "strange" and out of control. "They came to take charge of him because people were saying he had gone mad." (Mark 3:21) Apparently, his family didn't find that hard to believe, so they came to get him. The response of Jesus, when he is told that his mother and brothers have come, seems harsh. I sense some anger that they would believe the stories about him. Instead of greeting them with open arms, he turns to his audience and asks, "Who is my mother, my brother, and my sister?"

Jesus uses the arrival of his family to remind us that salvation isn't based on connections or formulas. Salvation isn't based on family bonds, tribal unity, group membership, or even religious practice. Only one thing matters: becoming fully who we are and giving that to God. A gift of less than ourselves will not work. "Son/daughter, give me your heart," is always God's command, God's recommendation, and God's invitation. "Whoever does the will of God is my brother, sister, and mother." So the response of Jesus isn't a rejection – it's an invitation. It's an invitation to expand our vision, to redefine ourselves. It's an invitation to become his relative, to be his family.

If there is any "formula" for salvation, it is in saying "yes" to Jesus. It is doing God's will, and living as Jesus' brother or sister. It is becoming one with him. Our "yes" must therefore be more than words we say or rituals we perform; our "yes" must be expressed in the life we live. We must become Jesus' relative; we must give him our heart. And we can do that, even though we may doubt, or fear, or fail... we can do that, even if we do not know his name.

How will you say "yes" to Jesus today?

The Sign Of Jonah   Luke 11:29

While still more people gathered in the crowd, he said to them, "This generation is an evil generation; it seeks a sign, but no sign will be given it, except the sign of Jonah."

In this passage, the Pharisees ask Jesus for a sign, as proof that he is from God. And yet signs were all around them. Jesus had just multiplied the loaves – the crumbs still clung to their lips – and still they asked for a sign!

We aren't so different from the ancient Israelites or Pharisees in our obsession with "signs" – how often do we make them a condition of our faith? The people in the time of Jesus taunted him to "come down off that cross; then we will believe!" And even today, we may say things like "Give me what I ask for in prayer, Lord, then I will believe! Then I will have faith in you!" In other words: do things *my* way; then I will believe! Do something flashy. Answer my prayers, make my life easy. Speak to one more prophet. Give me my miracle – then I will believe!

And yet God's own Son walked among us, and told us he would be with us always. He multiplied the loaves, walked on water, and even rose from the dead – and still we ask for a sign!

Our preoccupation – then and now – with "signs and wonders" says more about our need for excitement and certainty than it does about God's ability or willingness to provide such marvels. Indeed, it's remarkable how quickly we will pay attention to events when someone claims they've seen a vision or heard voices; multitudes will gather at such places without benefit of official sanction from the Church, and often without firm substantiation of the claim.

I suppose there is no harm in this, if such places and claims help bring us closer to God. But I think we might do well to ask ourselves why we have such a need for these "signs"! Is it our desire for security, for some "certainty" of God's presence in our uncertain world? Does our need for knowledge of the future through supposed "prophesies" give us the illusion that we can control our fate? And do these desires and needs reflect a lack of faith and trust in the words of Jesus? After all, everything we need for our salvation has already been revealed to us! There will be no "new" message, no "new" revelation. And the message Jesus brought to us will always be the same: trust in God, repent, and love!

Jesus didn't particularly want people to be dazzled by his miracles; he wanted them to hear and embrace his message. He must have worried that his "signs" might overshadow his words – which often led him to warn people to "say nothing to anyone about this" after a healing. He is obviously impatient with the Pharisees in this passage and flatly refuses to "perform on command," instead telling them, "The only sign you will get is the sign of Jonah!"

The prophet Jonah was upset because the people in Nineveh had repented and God didn't destroy them (it seems we don't have much tolerance for those who come late to the vineyard!). Then a tree sprouts in the desert and gives Jonah shade. Jonah realizes that he did nothing to "earn" the shade; he didn't "merit" the tree. It was God's free gift, just as mercy was God's gift to the people of Nineveh.

We, too, have the "sign of Jonah": a tree sprouting in the desert – an unearned gift, freely given. Grace overflowing! Mercy without limit! Forgiveness for the asking! Love without measure! Salvation, if we accept it!

"The only sign you will get is the sign of Jonah!"

Why is that not enough?

When Winter Comes

James R. Welter

~ Your Reflection ~

Born Again   *John 3:16*

"For God so loved the world that he gave his only Son, so that everyone who believes in him might not perish but might have eternal life."

My first job out of high school brought me to Chicago. "You must be born again!" a preacher on Wells Street screamed at me one day. I couldn't get a word in edgewise; he assured me that I was going to Hell as he continued to thump his Bible, banging out the "good news" of damnation!

I'm sure the most quoted verse is scripture is John 3:16; it's certainly the favorite verse of my fundamentalist friends. To them, it's the "formula" for salvation. And they insist it's the *only* one, and that I must subscribe to it. (Of course, there are those Catholics who get equally upset if their favorite devotion doesn't speak to me, or if my interpretation of scripture challenges them.) It's ironic to me that so many who quote John 3:16 have fallen into the same trap from which Jesus is trying to free Nicodemus (see John 3:1-21).

Nicodemus was a good man, a "closet disciple" of Jesus. He was a seeker of truth, so he came to Jesus in the dead of night. Nicodemus was also a "leader of the Jews," "a teacher of Israel" (John 3:10). Yet he has a hard time understanding Jesus. He is a prisoner of his obsession with the letter of the law. He is a prisoner of his attitude that it "must" be a certain way – *his* way. He had the "formula!"

When Winter Comes
James R. Welter

So when Jesus spoke of rebirth, that one must be "born again" to enter the kingdom of God, Nicodemus could only understand it one way... literally. A physical rebirth? That's impossible! *No*, Jesus responds – someone who is reborn spiritually knows the experience as surely as one who has been refreshed by an invisible breeze. How can a respected rabbi among the Jews not know this?

But Nicodemus doesn't know this, because his focus on "the law" has blinded him to other possibilities. His devotion to "the formula" has trapped him – he thinks that God can only work in the ways that *he* understands and expects. And we, too, may often fall into the "trap" of thinking that God can only save those who know our "formula": those who interpret scripture as I do; those who memorize the Catechism; those who speak the right words, go to the right church, or perform the proper rituals; those who follow *our* preferred path of faith.

But Jesus says: "Get out of your comfort zone, Nick! God is bigger than any box you can draw. So imagine something new!

Jesus says that only those who are "born again" can enter God's kingdom. So today, get out of *your* comfort zone! God is bigger than any box you can draw! Cast your net on the other side of the boat! Experience God in a new way! Believe! Walk on water!

Be born again!

My Demons, My Friends   Luke 4:33-34

In the synagogue there was a man with the spirit of an unclean demon, and he cried out in a loud voice, "Ha! What have you to do with us, Jesus of Nazareth? Have you come to destroy us?"

I have seen you in the temple and I shriek, "Have you come to destroy us, Jesus of Nazareth?" Destroy my demons?! My friends?! They have been with me always: those fears that enslave me, those relationships that bind me, those possessions that secure me, those hatreds that fill me. What do you want, Jesus of Nazareth? What will you ask of me? I fear your cure more than I fear my demons… my friends.

"Be quiet!" you command us! You hold me so gently, gaze at me with such compassion. Let go of me, you Hound of Heaven, you ever-pursuing one! You are always standing at my door. Calling to me from the beach. Gazing at me across the fields. Walking toward me at the temple. Turning to me on the mountain. What is it you ask of me? What is it you offer to me? To come? To follow? To belong? To leave all? To let go? To be free? You ask me to believe. You invite me to trust. You offer me hope. You give me love.

You hold me captive. You set me free.

Cast out my demons, that I may follow you, my Savior.

My friend.

When Winter Comes
James R. Welter

~ Your Reflection ~

Tell Me Your Name   Mark 5:6-9

Catching sight of Jesus from a distance, he ran up and prostrated himself before him, crying out in a loud voice, "What have you to do with me, Jesus, Son of the Most High God?   I adjure you by God, do not torment me!" [He had been saying to him, "Unclean spirit, come out of the man!"] He asked him, "What is your name?"

On my desk one Friday morning was a list of ten ways to "Get more productivity from a parish secretary." Item two was underlined: call them by name! A quick glance into the Pastor's office revealed that he too had been "blessed" with this list! I returned to my office with an ever-so-slight smirk of superiority. After all, he's the Pastor – he's supposed to be good at this "personal recognition" stuff. I'm an accountant; people expect me to be a "nerd"!

Knowing someone's name gives us power. I certainly learned this in sales: I saw salespeople lose deals (and clients) because they didn't get the name right. This idea of names giving power was prevalent in the ancient world, too – so when Jesus encounters the demon, the first thing he asks is "What is your name?" He then has power over the demon and expels it. It's interesting that, when Moses asks God his name in Exodus, God sidesteps the question and says, "I AM." In a comic routine, Bill Cosby has Moses ask, "I AM?! What kind of a name is that?!" But actually, it's not a name at all. It's a message from God, saying: "You don't have power over me. You can't control me. I'm God and you're not!"

When Winter Comes
James R. Welter

In this passage, Jesus encounters a tormented man. This "demoniac" was a powerful and frightening force in his community – no one in that territory was strong enough to tame or control him. So Jesus does what no one else was able to do – he overpowers the demons, expels them from the man, and sends them into a herd of swine. The swine then go over a cliff and drown in the lake. The community is saved; the good guys win! So how is Jesus rewarded for his good deed? They ask him to leave town! Why would they do this to someone who cast the demons out of an uncontrollable man? Maybe they were frightened by his obvious power. Maybe they decided that all they had done was exchange one person they couldn't control for *another* person they couldn't control!

Or maybe it was the owner of the herd, whose assets were suddenly depleted. Maybe he realized that it wasn't a "freebie" – maybe he realized that an encounter with Jesus was going to cost him something. He had to sacrifice something important to him – some of his material possessions – to have Jesus expel the demons. Maybe that was more than he bargained for. Maybe he decided that the price of the salvation Jesus offered was too high.

Are you ready to give Jesus *your* name? Are you ready to give him power over you? Are you ready for his salvation? Are you ready for him to rid you of the "demons" that torment you?

Are you ready to pay the price?

The Fourth Chapter:
See With New Eyes

When Jesus meets Bartimaeus, who is obviously blind, he asks a very strange question: "What do you want me to do for you?" One would expect that, upon seeing the man's blindness, Jesus would simply have healed him. But Jesus didn't presume to know the man's request. Instead, he takes the time to engage the man, not making any assumptions. He gives the man respect and dignity by taking the time to ask, and allowing the man to express his need.

That's the difference between Jesus and me. I label; Jesus listens. I assume; Jesus asks. I see the man's blindness; Jesus sees his faith.

"What do you want me to do for you?"

Lord, that I may see as you see. That I may see with new eyes.

Change   Acts 17:19-23

*They took him and led him to the Areopagus and said,
"May we learn what this new teaching is that you speak of?
For you bring some strange notions to our ears; we should like
to know what these things mean." Now all the Athenians as
well as the foreigners residing there used their time for nothing
else but telling or hearing something new.*

Then Paul stood up at the Areopagus and said:

*"You Athenians, I see that in every respect you are very reli-
gious. For as I walked around looking carefully at your shrines,
I even discovered an altar inscribed, 'To an Unknown God.'
What therefore you unknowingly worship, I now proclaim to
you."*

Change is difficult for most people. When it comes to
things centered on religion or tradition, there is often even
more resistance. Church humor captures that attitude:
"How many parishioners does it take to change a light bulb?"
"Change?! My grandfather donated that light bulb to
the church!"

The wisdom of the ancients was especially important to
the Greeks. So, speaking at Athens, Paul knew that anything presented as "new" would be heard and then quickly
dismissed. So Paul meets his listeners where they are – he
speaks in words they can understand. Normally, Paul is
direct, to the point of being a wild-eyed zealot: he usually
says, in effect, "Here's the Gospel of Jesus Christ; take it or
leave it." But here he is subtle, because he knows his audience. And so, to the Athenians, he says, "Your 'Unknown

When Winter Comes

James R. Welter

God' is who I'm talking about; this is nothing new." And he waits until the very end to spring the "R-word" on his audience – Resurrection! He takes them from where they are to where he wants them to go. Even so, not many follow. Change is not easy; we tend to cling to the familiar.

I told my light bulb story one evening, when my wife and I were talking about how difficult it is for most people to accept change. "You have to leave Indianapolis to get to Cincinnati," she responded. (You didn't get the joke, did you, honey?!) I think she meant, "You have to leave where you are to get to where you're going."

With physical change, no one questions such a simple principle. But in emotional or psychological change, it's not as obvious or as easy. You can't cling to your fear *and* trust in God. You can't harbor resentment *and* be forgiven. You can't be selfish *and* love freely. You can't seek to control everything *and* be open to the Spirit. You can't serve God *and* money. You must let go of one in order to embrace the other. You have to leave Indianapolis to get to Cincinnati!

Lord! If only our inner journey could be as simple!

Swallow a Camel   Matthew 23:23-24

Jesus said: "Woe to you, scribes and Pharisees, you hypocrites. You pay tithes of mint and dill and cummin, and have neglected the weightier things of the law: judgment and mercy and fidelity. [But] these you should have done, without neglecting the others. Blind guides, who strain out the gnat and swallow the camel!"

St. Monica (331-387 A.D.) was born to a family in Tagaste, North Africa, and had a highly disciplined Christian upbringing. Her marriage to Patricius, who held an official position at Tagaste, was arranged. Although he came from a Christian community, Patricius was not baptized until 370 A.D. Patricius' mother, who also lived with them, became a Christian because of St. Monica's influence. St. Monica is more widely known because of her prayers for her son, Augustine. Although St. Monica had other children, it was Augustine for whose conversion she would spend most of her life praying.

In this passage, Jesus again rips into the Pharisees for their obsession with "the rules." In the above passage, he utters two more (from a list of seven) "woes" to the scribes and Pharisees. The Pharisees put unnecessary burdens on others while neglecting to show charity, especially to the weak and the poor. They meticulously went through the correct motions of conventional religion, but neglected such duties as charity and mercy – they remembered the rules, but missed the message!

When Winter Comes

James R. Welter

Jesus used a humorous example to show how out-of-proportion their obsession with the "rules" had become. Gnats were considered the smallest of insects, and camels were considered the largest of animals in Palestine, and both were considered ritually impure. The scribes went to great lengths to avoid contact with gnats, even to the point of straining the wine cup with a fine cloth, lest they accidentally swallow a gnat. But Jesus says that, by missing the greater message of "the law," they were straining out the gnat but swallowing the camel!

It was so simple for Jesus! You don't need 615 laws – you don't even need ten! "Love God and love your neighbor." That's it!

Sometimes we get so obsessed with "the rules" – church law, canon law, civil law, bylaws – that we, too, forget their purpose. We miss the message! We "throw out the baby with the bath water." Or, as Jesus says, we "strain out the gnat and swallow the camel."

Saint Augustine (Monica's prayers were answered!) knew the freedom from "rules" that a true understanding of God's love and commandments could bring. His phrase was, "*Ama et fac quod vis.*" – Love, and do what you please.

With whom will you share your love today?

Just BE   Luke 10:38-42

[Jesus] entered a village where a woman whose name was Martha welcomed him. She had a sister named Mary [who] sat beside the Lord at his feet listening to him speak. Martha, burdened with much serving, came to him and said, "Lord, do you not care that my sister has left me by myself to do the serving? Tell her to help me." The Lord said to her in reply, "Martha, Martha, you are anxious and worried about many things. There is need of only one thing. Mary has chosen the better part and it will not be taken from her."

I like to think that I have grown to the point that I don't label people – that I see in each person a unique blend of gifts and talents.

Yeah, that's what I *like* to think!

But the fact is that I pretty quickly put people into two categories: the "doers" (those who are task-oriented) and the so-called "visionaries" or "dreamers" (I used to call them "blue-sky" or "cloud" people, but that got me into trouble!). A more scriptural label would be the "Marthas" and "Marys" of the world.

Jesus loved to visit the home of Martha and Mary and enjoyed their warm hospitality. In the brief encounter in Luke's gospel, we see two very different temperaments in Martha and Mary. Martha (the task-oriented person) loved to serve, but in her anxious manner of waiting on Jesus, she caused unrest. Mary, in her simple and trusting manner, waited on Jesus by just sitting attentively at his feet. She instinctively knew that what the Master wanted most at that moment was her presence. He just wanted her to "be" with him.

Every "Martha" wonders how dinner would get fixed if everyone chose to just "sit at the feet of Jesus" and "be"! Of course, the "Marthas" of the world are necessary – every committee must have a few, or else nothing will get done! The problem isn't in what Martha is doing; rather, it's in her motivation and attitude. Like her sister Mary, Martha was trying to get the attention of Jesus, and Martha's approach was to prepare a super-elegant meal. She was working overtime to pull it off, but it wasn't working – neither Jesus nor Mary was paying any attention.

So Martha "pretends" that she needs Mary's help in the kitchen. (We know she was pretending, because we "task-oriented" people always feel we can do things better ourselves!) "Tell her to help me," is a thinly veiled way of saying, "Look at what I'm doing here!" It seems Martha has a self-esteem problem: she sees little value in herself, and instead gets her sense of worth from what she does. So she is always "doing" something. She isn't really in touch with her true self, and so she fails to be in touch with Jesus.

It is always easier to blame someone else for our problems than to look inside ourselves, so she points the finger at her sister: "She's not helping! She's not buying into my need!

Tell her to help." But Jesus says, "Martha, Martha – you are anxious and worried about many things. There is need of only one thing." And that is to "be" with God in the present moment. Jesus implies that Martha is to forget the dinner and come and "be" with him and Mary, and deep down, that is what Martha wants and needs. And so, "Mary has chosen the better part" – Mary has taken the time to "be."

Constant anxiety and preoccupation keep us from being ourselves – from being fully human. They keep us from listening and being present to one another, and they keep us from being present to the Lord.

Take some time today to slow down and listen... and to simply "be" with Jesus.

~ Your Reflection ~

When Winter Comes   James R. Welter

~ Your Reflection ~

Clean Hands   Luke 11:37-40

After he had spoken, a Pharisee invited him to dine at his home. He entered and reclined at table to eat. The Pharisee was amazed to see that he did not observe the prescribed washing before the meal. The Lord said to him, "Oh you Pharisees! Although you cleanse the outside of the cup and the dish, inside you are filled with plunder and evil. You fools! Did not the maker of the outside also make the inside?"

As I read the gospel stories, I often wonder why anyone ever invited Jesus to dinner – he embarrasses or offends his hosts on a regular basis! After hearing Jesus preach, a Pharisee invited him to dinner. No doubt he invited Jesus because he wanted to hear more from this extraordinary man who spoke the word of God as no one else had ever done before. It was not unusual for a rabbi to give a teaching over dinner. Jesus, however, did something that offended his host – he did not perform the ceremonial washing of hands before beginning the meal.

Obviously, Jesus didn't just *forget* to wash his hands! Jesus was a creative and effective teacher, and he was already setting up the lesson. It was a masterful way to get the guests' attention, draw them into his teaching, and dramatize his point. The rabbi had been invited to dinner; perhaps they were thinking it would be good entertainment for the evening. But the host and guests got more than they bargained for – they had underestimated how good Jesus was at teaching, and I'm sure they never forgot the lesson (I'm also sure Jesus never got invited back!).

When Winter Comes

"Oh, you noticed that I didn't wash my hands?" he seems to say. "So which do you think is more important to God: clean hands or a clean heart? You know how to clean your hands; now let me tell you how to clean your heart! Love. Be merciful. Give alms!"

I knew it! I just knew he would ask for money sooner or later; preachers always do. We hear it all the time: "All the Church wants is money." But deep down, we know that's a "cop-out." It's not really about money; it's about letting go. And it's not about the preacher – it's about us. It's about our need to open our hands. It's about our need to give. When we give freely and generously, we express love. When we give in love, we express compassion, kindness, and mercy. And, if our heart is full of love and compassion, there is no room for greed, pride, envy, bitterness, or arrogance. Then we can eat with a clean heart, as well as clean hands.

"Thanks for the dinner invitation," I can hear Jesus saying at the end of the evening. "Oh, and one more thing: I didn't come to entertain you tonight – I came to change your life!"

You Don't Know Me   Hosea 11:3-4

Yet it was I who taught Ephraim to walk,
*   who took them in my arms;*
I drew them with human cords,
*   with bands of love;*
I fostered them like one
*   who raises an infant to his cheeks;*
Yet, though I stooped to feed my child,
*   they did not know that I was their healer.*

The green Baltimore Catechism books of the pre-Vatican world were written in question-and-answer form, and our Catechism classes in the 1950s consisted almost entirely of an effort to memorize the answers in the book. It was a pretty black-and-white approach: there was no doubt, discussion, hedging, or uncertainty in the answers that the catechism provided. These were *the answers* — period. The book's picture of Jesus with his arms around a sinner, above the caption "Jesus loves you WHEN you are sorry for your sins," didn't help much either. It was pretty easy to develop an image of a stern and legalistic God.

In Catechism class, I was Sister Gabriel's prize student. I always knew the answers, and I came from that experience knowing all about God. Yes, I knew all "about" God… yet I did not *know* God. I was well into adulthood before I could even bring myself to pray to God as "Father." Surely, I am one for whom Hosea writes: *"Yet, though I stooped to feed my child, he did not know me"* (paraphrase mine).

71

When Winter Comes
James R. Welter

It is summer, 1967. The visiting room of the state hospital in Logansport, Indiana, is stark. Sound echoes from the plain tile floor. Voices return from the bare walls. My father has been in this place for twenty-five years now. We are visiting today. The hushed quiet is broken, as a woman enters the room pushing a wheelchair. In it, she transports the deformed and helpless body of her son. Her eyes meet mine. Her pain outweighs my own; her son is my age. I turn away. They sit near us. This young man has a twin brother, who is perfectly normal. There is another brother, too, and a sister. But they have not seen this plain floor, these bare walls. They do not come to visit. But this mother has driven sixty-five miles today. She has driven sixty-five miles every Saturday, for sixteen years, to be with her son.

Her cross is especially heavy this day. Her son is restless, and she struggles to feed him. Suddenly, he knocks the tray from her hands. Mashed potatoes and gravy cover his clothes. Meatloaf slides to the floor; the green beans add a strange color. Only a mother knows. She begins to clean him up, as she must have done a thousand times before. Quietly, she sobs. And I hear her whisper to her son: "I gave you life. I have fed you all these years. I love you. And you don't even know me!"

I wonder how often God, our loving Father, could say that of us: "I gave you life... I have fed you all these years... I love you... and you don't even know me."

How will you seek to know God today?

Lord, That I May See   Luke 18:35-41

Now as he approached Jericho a blind man was sitting by the roadside begging, and hearing a crowd going by, he inquired what was happening. They told him, "Jesus of Nazareth is passing by." He shouted, "Jesus, Son of David, have pity on me!" The people walking in front rebuked him, telling him to be silent, but he kept calling out all the more, "Son of David, have pity on me!" Then Jesus stopped and ordered that he be brought to him; and when he came near, Jesus asked him, "What do you want me to do for you?" He replied, "Lord, please let me see."

The crowd in Luke's gospel was annoyed with the persistent shouts of the blind man, Bartimaeus (whose name is given in Mark 10:46-52). He was disturbing their peace and interrupting the talk Jesus was giving while making his way through town. It was common for a rabbi to teach as he walked with others, and Jesus was on his way to celebrate the Passover in Jerusalem, with a band of pilgrims following him. When the crowd tried to silence the blind man, he overwhelmed them with his emotional outburst and thus caught the attention of Jesus. The man knew that this was a once-in-a-lifetime opportunity, and he could not pass it up. He knew who Jesus was and must have heard of his fame for healing, but until now, he had no way of making contact with him. And now he was determined to get near the one person who could meet his need.

When they finally meet, Jesus asks a strange question: "What do you want me to do for you?"

When Winter Comes

James R. Welter

Hey, Jesus, here's a quarter – buy a clue! Can't you see that the guy's blind? When I pass a panhandler on the street with his basket out, I can flip him a dollar without even breaking stride; I certainly don't have to ask him what he wants from me!

But maybe that's the difference. On hearing and seeing the blind man, Jesus didn't presume to know the man's request. He didn't simply cure his blindness without a thought; he didn't just "flip him a dollar." Instead, he took the time to recognize and engage the man. He didn't make assumptions; he treated the man with dignity and respect by taking the time to ask about his problem, and allowing the man to express his need.

That's the difference between me and Jesus: I label; Jesus listens. I assume; Jesus asks. I see the man's blindness; Jesus sees his faith. I see his poverty; Jesus sees his potential. I see his filth; Jesus sees his fullness.

I judge. Jesus loves.

"What do you want me to do for you, Jim?"

"Lord, that I may see!"

Gathering Into Barns   Luke 12:16-19

*Then he told them a parable. "There was a rich man whose
land produced a bountiful harvest. He asked himself, 'What
shall I do, for I do not have space to store my harvest?'
And he said, 'This is what I shall do: I shall tear down my
barns and build larger ones. There I shall store all my grain
and other goods and I shall say to myself, 'Now as for you,
you have so many good things stored up for many years, rest,
eat, drink, be merry!'"*

We can learn a lot about the man in this parable by reading the text carefully. He came by his wealth honestly; the
passage says that "his" land bore good crops. He must
have worked hard; you don't get a good crop from the
drought-ridden farmlands of Palestine without hard work.
He got his wealth the old-fashioned way – he earned it!
And now he is tearing down his barns and building larger
ones to store his harvest, to provide for his family's future.
He doesn't seem like a bad person... and he's not. He is
one of us. He has worked hard all his life. One night he
puts his arm around his wife and says, "Honey, we've got it
made. The kids are out of college, and I'm only two years
from retirement. We have money in the bank, two nice
cars, and a condo in Florida. We've realized the American
dream – we've got a piece of the rock!" Then a voice comes
from heaven and says, "You fool, this night your life will be
required of you!"

The man in this story has much, but he does not have
an attitude of thankfulness. He attributes everything to

himself: *my* harvest, *my* barns, *my* goods. He remembers the gifts, but forgets the giver. And he forgets his neighbor, thinking only of himself. *I* have blessings in reserve for years to come, he says; I'll relax, eat heartily, drink well, and enjoy myself. He is self-reliant and self-centered. He's a "Lone Ranger Christian" – he asks for nothing and he gives nothing. He puts all of his security in what *he* has built, and thinks he is in control of his life!

Jesus had many wealthy friends, so it doesn't seem that he had a problem with wealth *per se* (although it's not what he chose for himself). The issues Jesus has are what kind of person we become as we accumulate our wealth, the things we do protect it, and the security we place in it.

It's so easy for us to convince ourselves that the material "things" we have don't control us. We like to say that we could easily give them up, that we would be just as happy without them – but would we? *Do* we?

Is my lifestyle affected by the amount I give away to help other people? Am I willing to tear down even one of my "barns" and not build a new one? Am I willing to give up some of my luxuries, so that others can have necessities? To what lengths do I go to increase my income, maximize my wealth, better my lifestyle – and to what lengths will I go to keep and protect those "things"?

And tonight, if my life is required of me... what kind of person will be standing before the Lord?

The Tenants Don't Own   Mark 12:1-3
The Vineyard

He began to speak to them in parables. A man planted a vineyard, put a hedge around it, dug a wine press, and built a tower. Then he leased it to tenant farmers and left on a journey. At the proper time, he sent a servant to the tenants to obtain from them some of the produce of the vineyard. But they seized him, beat him, and sent him away empty-handed."

In Jesus' time, the hills of Galilee were lined with numerous vineyards, and it was quite normal for the owners to lease their estates to tenants. Many did it for the sole purpose of collecting rent. The story Jesus told about the wicked tenants is a message of mercy and warning, and it tells us of God's generosity and trust. The vineyard is well-equipped with everything the tenants need; the owner then goes away and leaves the vineyard in the hands of the tenants. Similarly, God trusts us enough to give us the freedom to run our lives as we choose – with the warning that, one day, we will be called from our "vineyard" and held accountable.

In this gospel story, the problem is that the tenants refuse to give up the goods when the master's servant comes to collect. Instead, they beat him and send him away. They think that the produce belongs to them. They've started to believe that *they* own the vineyard!

When Winter Comes
James R. Welter

It's easy for us to fall under the same illusion – to think that we own the "vineyard" of our lives. Our society reinforces that attitude: it's all about you... you are what you have... get a piece of the rock! Accumulate "things" and you will be secure. So we build our big houses, protect ourselves in gated communities, and make judgments based on what others have – or don't have. We pretend that we've got it all, that we are in control, that things will never change, that the end will never come... because we own the vineyard!

I consider myself a "self-made man." I was one of seven kids raised by a single parent. I crawled across onion fields for fifteen cents an hour when I was seven, scratching to help make ends meet. I walked five miles into town each day to hold down a job during high school. (Our kids insist it was uphill both ways!) I don't remember anyone paying tuition for me, or pulling strings to get me a job. So it's easy for me to feel that what I have is mine. I earned it myself. I own the vineyard!

In my better moments, though, I remember that others were involved. Mom instilled in us a work ethic and a desire to break the poverty cycle. I recall a sixth-grade teacher who was a mentor to me. And I realize that my basic intelligence and ability is not the result of anything *I* have done. In truth, I didn't "do it all myself" – no one does.

In fact, everything I have is gift – from the Giver of all gifts. I am but a steward: I may lease the vineyard, but I *own* nothing! Our choice, then, is to live with open hands... or else learn the hard way, when the Master comes for us, that we *don't* own the vineyard!

Instead of acting as wicked servants, we must be responsible ones. So we thank you, Lord, for the privilege of working in your vineyard... *your* vineyard, not ours. And we pray, in the words of our American bishops: "May we receive your gifts gratefully, cherish and tend them in a responsible manner, share them in justice and love with others... and return them with increase to you."

~ Your Reflection ~

When Winter Comes
James R. Welter

~ Your Reflection ~

See With New Eyes

We Have Been   Luke 9:28-29, 32-33
To The Mountain

About eight days after he said this, he took Peter, John, and James and went up the mountain to pray. While he was praying his face changed in appearance and his clothing became dazzling white. Peter and his companions had been overcome by sleep, but becoming fully awake, they saw his glory and the two men standing with him. As they were about to part from him, Peter said to Jesus, "Master, it is good that we are here; let us make three tents."

One of our familiar hymns includes the line, "We'll just say we have been to the mountain / And caught a glimpse of all that we could be." I shared that line with my tour group as we traveled the Holy Land a few years ago. We were all struggling with how to describe our experiences: our experience of celebrating Eucharist on the sea of Galilee, of singing "How Great Thou Art" while standing at the garden tomb, of walking the Way of the Cross, and now standing on Mount Tabor. What will we tell them when we return? How can anyone who hasn't been here understand what it is like? When words fail, poetry speaks: "We'll just say we have been to the mountain… "

I don't think my wife and I have ever had a vacation during which one of us didn't say, "Let's not go back home; let's just stay here!" In this reading, Peter has had a good experience and he wants to stay. "Lord, it's good for us to be here. Let's build three tents!" But Jesus reminds him, "No, Peter – you can't stay in this special place.

When Winter Comes James R. Welter

You can't remain on vacation forever; you can't stay in a world where it's nice and safe. You've got to go back down the mountain. You've got to go back to your world, back to where you live and work. But when the going gets tough – when winter comes – remember what you have seen and heard today, and draw strength and comfort from it."

So when people ask why you don't accept the values of the world, just say you have been to the mountain!

When your health fails… when your parents grow old… when your child dies… when your pain is beyond the telling, yet your faith holds strong… just say you have been to the mountain!

And when it's your time to die… when they see no fear on your face… you'll just say you have been to the mountain – and caught a glimpse of all that you could be!

The Fifth Chapter:
Let Go, Let God

I hear you, Lord – knocking at my door. Why do I hesitate? Why do I not run to you?

Lord, forgive me for wanting to be the shepherd instead of the sheep. Forgive me for wanting to control my life, for thinking that I own your vineyard. Forgive me for holding on so tightly. Forgive me for not trusting you; for not having the courage to step out of the boat.

I hear you, Lord – knocking at my door. Why do I fear?

What is it you ask of me? What is it you offer me? To come? To follow? To belong? To leave all? To let go? To be free?

You ask me to believe. You invite me to trust. You offer me hope. You give me love.

I hear you, Lord – knocking at my door.

84

Grief   Matthew 17:22-24

As they were gathering in Galilee, Jesus said to them, "The Son of Man is to be handed over to men, and they will kill him, and he will be raised on the third day." And they were overwhelmed with grief.

When they came to Capernaum, the collectors of the temple tax approached Peter and said, "Doesn't your teacher pay the temple tax?"

It's 1967. I am a young man. We are at the funeral home where my father lies in state. It's my first experience with the death of a loved one. I look out the window and see cars passing on the street; people going to the grocery, running errands, living life – as if nothing has happened. I want to scream at them, "Hey! What are you doing?! My father is dead in here!"

My father was institutionalized for the last twenty-five years of his life. We missed all those growing up years together: the father-son talks, playing catch in the backyard, and a thousand other things. There are so many words we did not speak, so many songs we did not sing.

When we are opened up by a major loss, all the unattended-to grief of our life is opened up as well. Often this grief comes from the day-to-day losses and disappointments we all experience. Society doesn't give us permission to grieve the loss of friends moving, relationships ending, opportunities missed, rejections suffered, and failures experienced. So these minor hardships come bubbling to the top, spilling over, mixing with the grief of our traumatic loss.

When Winter Comes

James R. Welter

Grief doesn't usually take away our faith, but it often takes away our balance. It can lead to an overall sense of sadness that casts a shadow over our perception and experience of everything else. It can, at times, lead to an edgy defensiveness that protects our fragile spirit by shouting at others: "Don't mess with me!" The grief that comes from some trauma or devastating loss can so paralyze us that our reaction to everything is dulled, and our ability to respond to anything or anyone is severely affected. "Hey!" we want to shout, "My father is dead in here!"

In this passage from Matthew, the disciples are overwhelmed with grief when Jesus tells them that he's going to die in Jerusalem. This is followed by a strange little story about the temple tax. The Apostles must have wanted to scream, "Our friend has just told us he's going to die and you want our taxes?!" But Jesus doesn't make a big deal out of it. Life goes on, he seems to suggest. You still have to buy groceries, you still have to run errands, you still have to pay your taxes. But he knows the disciples are fragile. As if to show them that they must rely on God in times of disorientation and grief, he has them miraculously "find" the temple tax.

Jesus invites us to be gentle and patient with our grief. Can you peacefully name your sadness, your losses, and your disappointments? Can you quietly turn them over to the Lord so they do not weigh you down or throw you off balance?

Be at peace, Jesus says. Be at peace.

Eye of a Needle   Matthew 19:23-26

Then Jesus said to his disciples, "Amen, I say to you, it will be hard for one who is rich to enter the kingdom of heaven. Again I say to you, it is easier for a camel to pass through the eye of a needle than for one who is rich to enter the kingdom of God." When the disciples heard this, they were greatly astonished and said, "Who then can be saved?" Jesus looked at them and said, "For human beings this is impossible, but for God all things are possible."

Scholars differ as to the meaning of the "eye of a needle" to which Jesus refers in this passage from Matthew. I favor the interpretation that says Jesus is using hyperbole when he speaks of passing through the eye of a needle – that he doesn't mean it literally. Rather, he is using an exaggeration to suggest that one could sooner pass a camel through that tiny opening than one could get a rich man to enter God's kingdom. Others point out that in the time of Jesus, there was a low, narrow gateway into the city of Jerusalem called the "eye of the needle." It was designed to slow visitors' entry into the city. It functioned something like an airport's security checkpoint – it facilitated crowd control and protected against armed attack. This gateway, it is sometimes suggested, is what Jesus is referring to in this passage. It is difficult, but not impossible, to pass a camel through it. But, to pass through the "eye of the needle," the camel's rider had to dismount and unburden himself and his camel of all goods, wealth, and possessions. One couldn't pass through that narrow gateway carrying a bunch of "stuff"! Those who were unwilling to "let go" and so unburden themselves could not pass through the gateway and enter the city. In either interpretation, Jesus seems to be implying that it is the rich person's greed and selfish desire for wealth that keeps him from entering the Kingdom of God.

To capture monkeys in Africa, I'm told, the native people attach a small cage to a tree. The cage is just big enough to hold a banana. The monkey reaches through the bars and grabs the banana, but when the monkey tries to withdraw his prize, the banana won't fit through the bars and the monkey is trapped! Ironically, all the monkey has to do to escape is open his hand and let go of the banana. Let go of his possession. Let go of his greed. Let go of that which holds him captive.

In the same way, Jesus suggests that to pass through the eye of the needle and enter God's kingdom, all we have to do is open our hands! All we have to do is let go of the banana! Let go of our possessions, our greed, our selfishness. Let go of those things that hinder our growth. Let go of those things that hold us captive. Let go of all those things that keep us away from God.

To what are you clinging today? What keeps you from entering God's kingdom? Jesus says, "With God, all things are possible." So, with God, you can let go of those "things." With God, you can open your hands. With God, you can pass through the eye of a needle!

With God, you can enter the kingdom!

It Hurts To Move   Genesis 12:1

The LORD said to Abram: "Go forth from the land of your kinsfolk and from your father's house to a land that I will show you."

I love to take vacations and travel, but I don't like to move: my wife and I have lived in the same city, on the same street, in the same house, for almost 30 years. I like the prospect of a stable "home," a place to settle. This idea is very appealing to me, and not just in the physical sense of a location – a certain city, street, or house. I mean that the *idea* is appealing, because it is much easier for me to simply stay where I am than it is for me to meet the challenge of going outside my parameters of comfort and familiarity. It is easier to stay in one place than to "move" to a new place, to get a new map, to learn and relearn where things are, how I am supposed to act, what is expected of me, and where I can find solace and safety when I need it.

The example of Abram, however, challenges me to make the unknown my "home." The medieval mendicants knew that they would never truly be "home" in this life, so they made the road their "home." Similarly, an old tradition holds that the followers of Jesus should "be passers-by" in the world, always keeping in mind that their "home" and destination lie elsewhere. After all, a Christian is a believer on pilgrimage – a person on mission, someone who is going somewhere unknown, to places (as the *Star Trek* television series puts it) "no one has gone before."

When Winter Comes James R. Welter

As a Christian, I want to be someone who never gets too comfortable in the world. I want to be willing to walk into situations of uncertainty and darkness, and try to light a candle. I want to be able to "move" from my present position when necessary – intellectually, spiritually, and physically. I want to be a person who is free enough to admit when I am wrong, and free enough to grow, learn, and to change. I want to be like a child, exploring the world and living in it freely and wholeheartedly, yet never become distracted from my purpose.

All these things I want to be. But instead, I often find myself crying to my Father, echoing the words of our five-year-old son when his childhood friend moved away: "Daddy, it *hurts* to move!"

God's Time   John 8:28-30

So Jesus said [to them], "When you lift up the Son of Man, then you will realize that I AM, and that I do nothing on my own, but I say only what the Father taught me. The one who sent me is with me. He has not left me alone, because I always do what is pleasing to him." Because he spoke this way, many came to believe in him.

Three days after my high school graduation, I left "hayseed" Indiana with sixteen of my classmates to join the Navy and see the world. At boot camp, those "city slickers" from Chicago made fun of us farm boys when we saw our first subway and gasped, "You mean that train goes under the ground?!" But we got our revenge when *they* saw their first cow. We took delight in explaining to them where milk comes from! There was a collective "yuuuck!" but we assured them it was the "udder" truth!

It takes a lot of faith and trust to make a living on a farm. Planting in the spring requires trust — trust that the frosts are gone, trust that the sun won't be too hot, trust that the rains will come at the right times. And if the rains do not come, it takes a lot of faith to plant again the next year with the same expectations. It's all in God's hands. It's all in God's time.

There are many readings in scripture that speak of trust and living by God's time. Shadrach, Meshach, and Abednego trusted in their God; they said that they would remain faithful even if God did not help them. They said they would believe in God even if he was silent. Martha and Mary, the sisters of Lazarus, trusted in God – but they had to wait on God's time. Susanna trusted in God's promises, and God rescued her at the last moment. Joseph trusted God, and accepted the pregnant Mary into his home.

These stories are present in scripture to teach us to have faith in God's promises. They show us what happens when we trust in the Lord and wait on God's time. They teach us to be humble so that God can take over. Trust requires humility. It requires living in expectation, like the farmer. It requires us to be open, like a child. It requires us to be receptive, like the earth.

Like a good farmer, in planting our fields – in living our lives, in doing our work, in accepting our joys and sorrows – we have to trust and wait on God's time.

We must have faith… it's all in God's hands…

…the rains will come!

Jonah's To Do List   Jonah 3:1-5

The word of the LORD came to Jonah a second time: "Set out for the great city of Nineveh, and announce to it the message that I will tell you." So Jonah made ready and went to Nineveh, according to the LORD's bidding. Now Nineveh was an enormously large city; it took three days to go through it. Jonah began his journey through the city, and had gone but a single day's walk, announcing, "Forty days more and Nineveh shall be destroyed," when the people of Nineveh believed God; they proclaimed a fast and all of them, great and small, put on sackcloth.

I'm a task-oriented person (which is not a bad trait for an accountant!), and I like to work from a "to do" list. My "to do" list keeps me focused on my work and becomes a gauge for my day's success. One Tuesday afternoon, I was just three items away from a "successful" day when I saw *her* wandering around the Narthex. "Can I help you?" I asked. "I need to see a priest," the woman replied. (I had seen that coming!) "The Pastor is on retreat and it's the Associate's day off today," I informed her. (It never fails, I thought!) "But you can make an appointment…" "I need to talk to someone now," she said. (I had seen that coming, too!)   As I took her back to my office, I thought, "Two quick food vouchers and a gas ticket, and I'll be able to get back to my work."

It soon became apparent that the woman's financial need was far beyond our capacity, and her legal needs beyond my expertise. I listened to her for a long, long time, and offered her a few suggestions. Just before she left, she hugged me like she never wanted to let go... and I whispered to her of God's love.

In this passage, Jonah has plans: he has his own "to do" list, and it doesn't include going to Nineveh. We are told that it should have taken three days just to cover the territory, so big was Nineveh. But after a single day of work on Jonah's part, the *entire city* (an "enormously large city") repents in sackcloth and ashes! As is often the case with us, Jonah was brought to Nineveh kicking and screaming – it wasn't on his "to do" list to go there!

I can't imagine that it was Jonah's effective preaching, his way with words, or his enthusiasm that brought about the conversion of Nineveh. No, the Lord *wants* this city to be converted and the Lord brings it about, even through a reluctant mouthpiece. It's the power of the message, not the messenger, that brings about success. That's the "good news" about working in the Lord's vineyard – you don't have to be any good; you just have to show up and play! The "bad news" about it, of course, is that we must give up our previous plans – our own "to do" list, our self-centered goals and aspirations – in order to follow God's agenda.

For all Jonah's reluctance, in the end, he does exactly what he's told: he preaches God's message (not his own), in a place he'd really rather not be. Though a more willing spirit might be preferable, Jonah nevertheless provides all that is necessary for a successful mission in God's sight.

He does what God asks; he fulfills God's agenda. He follows God's "to do" list!

It was almost six o'clock when I returned to the work on my desk. I looked at the three items still on my "to do" list and mumbled, "Well, my list didn't get any shorter."

And God laughed, "Yes, but you got *mine* done!"

~ Your Reflection ~

When Winter Comes

James R. Welter

~ Your Reflection ~

Help My Unbelief!   Mark 9:20-24

They brought the boy to him. And when he saw him, the spirit immediately threw the boy into convulsions. As he fell to the ground, he began to roll around and foam at the mouth. Then he questioned his father, "How long has this been happening to him?" He replied, "Since childhood. It has often thrown him into fire and into water to kill him. But if you can do anything, have compassion on us and help us." Jesus said to him, "'If you can!' Everything is possible to one who has faith." Then the boy's father cried out, "I do believe; help my unbelief!"

The characters in this story approach Jesus the way we often do: how many times have we turned to God in prayer only when everything else has failed and we are at our wit's end? "If you can do anything, have compassion on us and help us." This is not expectant faith! And Jesus is incredulous: "'*If* you can!' Everything is possible to one who has faith!" And the father replies, "I do believe; help my unbelief!"

The cry of the boy's father is the cry we often give as we recognize the weakness of our own faith. We do our best to trust in God, yet tragedy and hardship all too often cause our faith to falter. Yet Jesus challenges the man in this story to pray boldly with faith and to expect a miracle: "Everything is possible to one who has faith!" St. Augustine, in his commentary on this passage, reminds us that prayer and faith go together: "Where faith fails, prayer perishes. For who prays for that in which he does not believe?"

When Winter Comes
James R. Welter

With the passage of time, one has the opportunity to look back on one's life – and it's often amazing how things seem to fit together. With hindsight, I can see God working in my life: this had to happen, so that could happen, and that's how I ended up here! Things have often turned out differently than I had planned, yet better than I had hoped. But even with the benefits of age and experience, I find that I am often no less hesitant to trust in the Lord when something new comes along; I am no more comfortable "letting go and letting God." For all my maturity, it doesn't seem that my level of trust has increased very much.

Of course I *want* to believe, and, like the father in today's reading, I say that I do believe. But when I'm called to let go – when I'm called to trust, when I'm called to love, when I'm called to believe that "all things work together for the good" – I falter. The sound of the wind distracts me; the lashing of the waves frightens me. My own fears and insecurities cause me to cling to the familiar, and the unknown road I may be asked to walk makes me tremble. Peter may step out – but, along with the other disciples, I stay in the boat!

I believe, O Lord. I believe.

Help my unbelief.

I'm God and You're Not   ***1 Samuel 3:6-7***
Again the LORD called Samuel, who rose and went to Eli. "Here I am," he said. "You called me." But he answered, "I did not call you, my son. Go back to sleep." At that time Samuel was not familiar with the LORD, because the LORD had not revealed anything to him as yet.

I sometimes get irritated with those folks who claim to have a "pipeline to God." They claim to hear God speaking to them in a very clear voice on a regular basis, and they claim to get specific instructions for their life. Maybe I'm just envious, because I tend to relate more to Samuel in this story. Samuel isn't sure that it's God's voice he hears; twice he assumes it is Eli's. It doesn't even occur to Samuel that God would call *him* – after all, Eli the priest is right there! I can relate to that: why would God use me? I'm an accountant, for goodness sake!

In the early days of *Saturday Night Live*, Chevy Chase would open the show with a classic line: "Good evening! I'm Chevy Chase, and you're not!" Why would you use an accountant, Lord, when there are so many others more qualified? I can hear the answer: "Because I'm God, and you're not!"

The awareness that God can use anyone he chooses came to me one day in the 1980s. I had developed a scripture program that presented the Catholic and mainline Christian approach to scripture interpretation, and I presented it in many parishes (as I still do, upon request).

When Winter Comes

James R. Welter

I didn't think of it as a "ministry" – it didn't occur to me that God might be at work; it was just something educational that I enjoyed doing.

A couple of years into it, I was invited to a parish where everything went wrong. No one had told the Pastor that I was to do a promotion at Sunday Mass – there were no committee members there to introduce me, and there was no sign-up table. I "faked it" and made it through, but decided that the whole thing wasn't fun anymore and resolved never to do the program again.

During the third of my weekly presentations there, some members of a scripture study group came to me. They told me that one of their members, an elderly lady named Opel, had really been struggling with what I was saying about God. She came from a fundamentalist background, and her experience of God was one of legalism and fear. She told their group that during the course of my program, for the first time in her life, she had come to know God as a loving Father. "That's really nice," I said. "I'd like to meet this lady!" "You can't," came the reply. "Opel died last night."

I was overwhelmed. I had a long, loud talk with God on the way home that night! "What are you doing, Lord?!" I yelled. "I was only having fun, and you send someone like her to *me!* Didn't you see those guys in black? They're priests! You're supposed to use them. Don't you know that I'm an accountant?!" "Jim," I perceived God to say, "I'm God, and you're not! I can use anybody I want, even an accountant. Even you!"

It is clear that, for whatever reason, God chooses very ordinary people to bring about his kingdom. Remember Peter's response when he was first called: "Depart from me, Lord, for I am a sinful man!" (Luke 5:8) Depart, nothing! Believe it or not, Pete, you're going to lead the charge!

Do you believe that God can use anybody… even you?

How will you let him use you today?

~ Your Reflection ~

When Winter Comes

James R. Welter

~ Your Reflection ~

The Sixth Chapter:
Faith and Trust

To walk on water, you've got to get out of the boat! At the invitation of Jesus, Peter got out of the boat. He left his comfort zone, and began walking on the water! But then he heard the wind and felt the lashing of the waves. Frightened, he began to sink.

Jesus calls us, too. We are challenged to leave our comfort zones, to stretch, to color outside the lines – to get out of the boat. We, too, are challenged to do that which seems impossible. We are challenged to walk on water.

When Peter listened to the voice of Jesus – when he listened to the invitation to "come" – he was able to do the impossible. But, when he listened to the sound of the wind and the waves, he faltered.

The message for us is clear: listen to the Voice!

God's Plan B   Matthew 11:25

At that time Jesus said in reply, "I give praise to you, Father, Lord of heaven and earth, for although you have hidden these things from the wise and the learned you have revealed them to the childlike."

When discussions turn to how God's will interfaces with our will, one of my favorite sayings is, "God always has a 'Plan B'." By that, I mean that I view God's knowledge like a giant computer game – but, unlike us, he knows all the possibilities and he determines how the game will turn out regardless of what choices I make or what "buttons" I may "push." In other words, although I am free to make my own decisions, God will go to "Plan B" to get his will done, based on *whatever* choices I make. As a Christian, I try to make prayerful choices and consider how I can best serve God's will. But it's comforting to know that I can't miss – that God will go to "Plan B" and find a way to use whatever I choose to do.

Old Testament readings take it a step further. In the book of Isaiah, for example, we are reminded that God makes use of people and events even when they have no intention of being a part of his plan, or are even in opposition to it. Clearly, in Isaiah 10:5-7, when the Assyrian ruler implements God's plan, what he achieves "is not what he intends." Cyrus certainly had no intention of being a part of God's plan when he repatriated the exiled Jews. And Caesar Augustus did not intend to further the divine plan when he decreed a census that resulted in Mary's child being born in Bethlehem of Judea. And the intentions of Judas and Pontius Pilate were to betray and execute Jesus — not to set the stage for the Resurrection!

The vision of faith operative in Scripture recognizes all of these actions as part of God's plan. Of course, the vision of faith does not change the data of experience, which is there for anyone — believer or non-believer — to see. But it changes *us*; it changes how we receive the information and the way in which we respond to it. Perhaps it is much like prayer, which does not so much "change God's mind" about the unfolding of events as it changes the heart of the one who, in praying, opens himself or herself to the divine will.

I don't pretend to know how all that works. But I think this gospel passage is telling us that human wisdom and learning alone will not reveal God's hand in our life — that we must somehow, in the words of one philosopher, go "beyond the rational" to see that.

Perhaps this is what Jesus means when he says, "Although you have hidden these things from the wise and the learned, you have revealed them to the childlike." In other words, to see the "big picture," we must have "childlike" characteristics: single-heartedness, trust, and an awareness of God's love. Our dependence on God's goodness is what allows us to see his hand at work in our life.

It's unbelievable... some would say! It's coincidence... some would say! It's a happy result from an unhappy event... some would say! And perhaps, in a sense, it is all these things – but Jesus promises more. The resurrected Christ doesn't just promise that good things will come from the bad stuff that happens... he promises that life will come from death. God *always* has a "Plan B."

How will you strive to follow God's plan today?

~ Your Reflection ~

When Winter Comes

James R. Welter

~ Your Reflection ~

Is God Enough?   Matthew 6:5-6

*"When you pray, do not be like the hypocrites, who love to
stand and pray in the synagogues and on street corners so that
others may see them. Amen, I say to you, they have received
their reward. But when you pray, go to your inner room, close
the door, and pray to your Father in secret. And your Father
who sees in secret will repay you."*

I couldn't believe the conversation: "The statement you
sent me didn't show how much I gave to the church
last year. It showed zero and I give every week!"
The parishioner on the phone was a little irate. "I don't
know how we could have missed recording your donation
every week," I replied. "We balance the envelopes against
the deposit..." "Envelopes?" There was surprise in her
voice. "I don't use envelopes – I give cash!" She went on
to explain that Jesus said you shouldn't "let your left hand
know what your right hand is doing." "Well, can I get a
tax statement?" she asked. "Uh... I guess you'll have to
talk to the Lord about that...!"

I always encourage people to use their weekly contribution
envelopes. Not only does this practice enable them to get a
tax statement for their contributions, but it also gives
witness to their support of our ministries and to their
belief in what we do as a church. We give witness to our
faith all the time – in everything from Lenten ashes to
public prayer meetings. But in this passage, Jesus challenges our motives: "Do not pray *for* others to see" – in
other words, merely to "look good" or to appear devout.

When Winter Comes
James R. Welter

Jesus says it is best to pray in secret, where only God knows. But is God enough for me? Is God enough, or do I need a big house and fancy car? Is God enough, or do I need expensive clothes and jewelry? Is God is enough, or do I build walls and lock gates to protect myself from those who have less than I? Is God is enough, or do I cling to my possessions? Is God enough, or do I chase after wealth, power, or fame? Is God enough, or do I avoid certain people for fear of what might be said about me?

If God is enough – why do I fear what he might ask of me?

In his poem "The Hound of Heaven," Francis Thompson gives voice to our fears: "I ran down the nights and down the days sore a'dread / if I had Him, I would have nothing else besides."

But the truth is, if we don't have God… it doesn't matter if we have *everything* else.

And, if we do have God… then we *need* nothing else!

Is God enough for you today?

Washing in the River 2 Kings 5:9-13

Naaman came with his horses and chariots and stopped at the door of Elisha's house. The prophet sent him the message: "Go and wash seven times in the Jordan, and your flesh will heal, and you will be clean." But Naaman went away angry, saying, "I thought that he would surely come out and stand there to invoke the LORD his God, and would move his hand over the spot, and thus cure the leprosy. Are not the rivers of Damascus, the Abana and the Pharpar, better than all the waters of Israel? Could I not wash in them and be cleansed?" With this, he turned about in anger and left.

But his servants came up and reasoned with him. "My father," they said, "if the prophet had told you to do something extraordinary, would you not have done it?"

As a young salesman, I had tried everything in the book to close a particular deal. Nothing worked. Then a guy came in from the "home office," said the same things to the client that I had said, and successfully closed the sale. "How did you do that?" I asked. "No magic," he said. "It's just that I'm from out-of-town and carry a briefcase!"

No prophet is accepted in his own land – the local sales rep just doesn't have the authority of "the guy from out-of-town with a briefcase!"

In the same way, we often don't recognize the miracles in our own backyard. In this passage, Naaman traveled far to visit the prophet Elisha and was healed. But the folks in the prophet's own town missed out: they just saw Elisha as "that guy down the street," the "local rep." He couldn't possibly know anything; he didn't even carry a briefcase! (I think I still have some issues about losing that sale…)

Naaman, for his part, wanted a flashy miracle – a little ritual and pageantry. But he was simply told to go and wash in the river! That seemed too ordinary. Wash in the river?! But I do that every day! His servants, however, had the right idea: they correctly pointed out that, if he had been told to do something extraordinary – if he had talked to that "guy from out-of-town with the briefcase" – he would have done what was asked without hesitation! But like us, Naaman wasn't looking for a miracle in the ordinary, everyday, "unremarkable" routine of life.

My wife, Helen, is a home health nurse. A few years ago, as she was driving through a rural area and making her rounds, she passed a road where one of her patients lived. "That patient isn't on my schedule today," she thought to herself, "but I think I'll just stop in and see how she's doing while I'm out this way." As she entered the house, the patient was choking – she had already turned blue. The patient's daughter was standing nearby, paralyzed with fear, unable to move. Helen's simple Heimlich maneuver saved the woman's life and spared the daughter untold guilt and sorrow.

We tend to expect miracles to be an interruption of nature – we expect them to be flashy and "magical" – and that expectation can keep us from seeing the miracles that   happen all around us, in ordinary life, as part of everyday events. What simple elements: a minor change in plans, a basic first-aid procedure, and a life is saved. Ordinary acts – performed in a miracle of timing!

If we only pay attention to the "unusual" events in our world – if we only believe "the guy from out-of-town with the briefcase" – we can miss the everyday miracles in our lives. We may miss the babies being born, the flowers blooming, the inspired words of our loved ones and friends. We may miss seeing God subtly at work in everyday events. Like the people in the gospels, we miss Jesus in our midst! We say with them, "That can't be the Messiah; that can't be Jesus…"

"…he looks just like us!"

When Winter Comes
James R. Welter

~ Your Reflection ~

Come and Stay At My Home   Acts 16:13-15

On the sabbath we went outside the city gate along the river where we thought there would be a place of prayer. We sat and spoke with the women who had gathered there. One of them, a woman named Lydia, a dealer in purple cloth, from the city of Thyatira, a worshiper of God, listened, and the Lord opened her heart to pay attention to what Paul was saying. After she and her household had been baptized, she offered us an invitation: "If you consider me a believer in the Lord, come and stay at my home."

One of the downsides of working for the Church or being involved in volunteer ministries is that you tend to expect more from people than you often get. For some people, the disillusionment involved in working in ministry is so great that they can't bring themselves to serve on certain committees; others leave church work, or even the Church itself, in disgust. As with Paul and the disciples, we are often stoned by the very people we seek to serve. Like many, I've been around long enough to know that if you put two human beings together, you will inevitably have politics, misunderstandings, false judgment, deception, agendas, and friction.

So, when these things happen in the Church, why do they seem so much more hurtful? I think it's because our expectations and hopes are so much higher. I used to have a penholder on my desk that depicted a man with a knife in his back slumped over his desk. The man standing over him was saying, "Sorry Charlie, but business is business." In the business world, there were no illusions: our goal was profit and our intentions of getting it were pretty clear. That may not have been admirable, but at least it was honest.

In our church life, we want more and we expect more. And so there is disappointment: after all, if people can't get along in the Church, how can they get along anywhere else? I often wonder why, in a church environment, we don't cut each other a little more slack. Shouldn't we be better than "the world"? In this passage from Acts, Lydia says: "If you consider me a believer in the Lord, come and stay at my house." If we are one in our faith, then "stay at my house" – talk to me, listen to me, trust me. Be open and honest with me. See goodness in me, and give me the benefit of the doubt. Enter into a relationship with me.

If we do not stem the tide – if we are no different than the world – then the gospel has a dire warning for us: "The hour is coming when everyone who kills you will think he is offering worship to God. They will do this because they have not known either the Father or me."

"If you consider me to be a believer in the Lord, come and stay at my home."

Whom will you invite into your "home" today?

Hang On   John 11:20-27

When Martha heard that Jesus was coming, she went to meet him; but Mary sat at home. Martha said to Jesus, "Lord, if you had been here, my brother would not have died. [But] even now I know that whatever you ask of God, God will give you." Jesus said to her, "Your brother will rise." Martha said to him, "I know he will rise, in the resurrection on the last day." Jesus told her, "I am the resurrection and the life; whoever believes in me, even if he dies, will live, and everyone who lives and believes in me will never die. Do you believe this?" She said to him, "Yes, Lord. I have come to believe that you are the Messiah, the Son of God ..."

My mother raised seven children alone on a broken-down old farm and was almost eighty-eight years old when she died in 1995. We had talked of death many times; she couldn't understand why she had lived so long. "Even the people I knew at the Senior Citizens Center have all died," she lamented one evening. Mom was ready to go.

Mom died on a Wednesday, the twelfth. As her funeral began on a January morning, all seven of us walked behind her casket into a little country church in Knox, Indiana. All seven of us had been baptized in that little church. All seven of us had received our first communion there, and been raised in the Catholic faith in that church. As we entered the church, we sang one of Mom's favorite old Baptist hymns: "Sweet hour of prayer / sweet hour of prayer / that takes me from this world of care."

When Winter Comes
James R. Welter

We laid Mom to rest in a little cemetery near our old farm. Her grave is next to that of our infant sister, who had died more than fifty years ago. The death of a parent has its own special grief. Mom's death was difficult, but it seemed "right"; it was the next normal step in life.

Eight weeks later, we were back in that little country church. This time we walked in behind the casket of my sister Fran. We sang that same hymn — but this time it didn't seem "right." This time every fiber of my being screamed, "Why, Lord?! Why my sister? Why Frannie? Why now, so soon after Mom?"

An out-of-sequence death has its own special pain. Martha screams for all of us: "If you had been here, Lord, my brother would not have died!" Jesus replies, "Your brother will rise." "I know, Lord, on the last day!" But Jesus looks into our eyes: I'm not talking about some nebulous future time! "I am the resurrection and the life." Today, your sister, your brother, your parent, your spouse, your child — lives! "Do you believe this?" Martha answers for all of us: I've never seen a life beyond this one; never known anyone to rise from the dead. This isn't in my experience. It hurts so much. It hurts so much. But she says, "I believe you are the Messiah." I believe in you!

When it feels like our very lives have been ripped from us — when our pain is beyond the telling — like Martha, all we can do is hold on: "I believe in you, O Lord. I believe in you!"

Wrestling With God   Genesis 32:24-27

After he had taken them across the stream and had brought over all his possessions, Jacob was left there alone. Then some man wrestled with him until the break of dawn. When the man saw that he could not prevail over him, he struck Jacob's hip at its socket, so that the hip socket was wrenched as they wrestled. The man then said, "Let me go, for it is daybreak."

There is only one way God ever gets me from "Point A" to "Point B" in my life – he drags me, kicking and screaming! So I can easily identify with Jacob in this story as he "wrestles with God!"

It always seems to me that if God wants me to get to "Point B," he should at least let me know what it is, and how I am supposed to get there. That doesn't seem like an unreasonable request! And if even a fraction of what we say about God (that he is the Creator of the world, all-knowing and all-powerful, etc.) is true, then we at least have to credit him with the ability to communicate!

It seems unlikely, then, that the problem is on *God's* end. We must therefore conclude that *we* have a "listening" problem! And that is where we "wrestle." We wrestle with distractions; there are many voices that tell us we aren't even looking in the right direction. We wrestle with darkness – the way doesn't seem clear. We wrestle with the sense that we are in this alone. We wrestle with the illusion that *we* know what is best. And we wrestle with temptations, to go another way or to simply give up.

When Winter Comes

James R. Welter

It just seems that being a Christian shouldn't have to be so difficult! Of course, there is no basis for us to expect otherwise: even Jesus was not spared doubt, temptation, conflict, or hardship. We see him again and again going into the desert – to pray, to struggle, to ponder, to seek – to "wrestle" with God. He faces temptation in the desert; he sweats drops of blood in the garden. Even with his final breath, he is still struggling to understand: "My God, my God, why have you forsaken me?"

But notice that, in this story, it was when Jacob dared to cross over the river that he prevailed in his contest with the heavenly being and received a new name. And for Jesus, the cross ultimately brought not defeat, but victory. For us, too, it is when we dare to enter "new territory" – to make new decisions, try new things, or begin a new life – that we are called to contend or "wrestle" with God. "Seeing God face-to-face" – that is, coming to understand God's will for us – is not merely a one-time thing. It is not an event, but a process – a "struggle." It is not a thing to *achieve*, but a thing for us to *choose* and *seek*... not once, but again and again and again.

Both the story of Jacob and the life of Jesus teach us that, if we remain faithful – if we persevere, if we continue to "struggle" with God – we will be rewarded. As with Jacob, as with Jesus, it is our "struggle" that will ultimately give us the strength to continue our journey of faith into the Promised Land. It is our "struggle" with God... that will bring us victory!

Mulberry Trees   Luke 17:5-6

And the apostles said to the Lord, "Increase our faith." The Lord replied, "If you have faith the size of a mustard seed, you would say to [this] mulberry tree, 'Be uprooted and planted in the sea,' and it would obey you."

When I was a kid on the farm, we hated mulberry trees. You could eat blackberries, strawberries, and blueberries – but mulberries were useless. We had a mulberry tree in our yard, right where we liked to play and run barefoot. And on the farm, there was only one thing worse to feel oozing between your toes than fallen mulberries…!

I was a daily Bible reader at age twelve. My father had been taken from us before I started school. Reading the Bible that I had found in my father's desk somehow seemed to put me in touch with him. This habit of reading the Bible developed into a lifelong interest in scripture. And I remember being elated when I first read this passage: "If you had faith the size of a mustard seed, you could say to this mulberry tree, 'Be uprooted and planted in the sea,' and it would obey you."

Wow! As a kid, I thought it would be really cool to make that mulberry tree move out of our yard and into the cow pasture! It would certainly impress my siblings and gain favor from Mom… and the Bible said I would be able to do it! So all afternoon and into the night I prayed, and repeated my belief that, in the morning, the tree would be banished into the cow pasture. The next morning I ran to the window, only to find the tree standing defiantly in the yard. "Yeah, just as I thought," I mumbled.

This experience taught me not to take scripture too literally. I realized that we must consider what the Bible "means," not just what it "says." In this passage, Jesus is not telling us how to clear unwanted timber from our yard – he is trying to express the power of faith. He is reminding us that God expects more from us than we can accomplish by ourselves, and that faith in God is the key for removing obstacles and overcoming difficulties in our lives. The "mulberry trees" are those challenges and difficulties we encounter that seem beyond our power to handle. But they are not beyond *God's* power!

"Yeah, just as I thought" isn't just a child's reaction; it often betrays a lack of faith. Faith is not "rational"! Faith doesn't "make sense," in the common meaning of the term. Faith is believing that God can and does work through us. Faith is leaving our comfort zone. Faith is "stepping out of the boat." Faith is listening to "the Voice." When Peter listened to the invitation of Jesus to "come," he was able to do the impossible and walk on water. But when he listened to the frightening sound of the waves, he faltered and sank.

The message for us is clear: when you listen to the Voice, you can do the impossible. You can move that mulberry tree into the sea! Today, don't tell God how big the "mulberry trees" in your life are – instead, tell those "mulberry trees" how big your God is! And have faith!

Back Home Again   Luke 2:46-49

After three days they found him in the temple, sitting in the midst of the teachers, listening to them and asking them questions, and all who heard him were astounded at his understanding and his answers. When his parents saw him, they were astonished, and his mother said to him, "Son, why have you done this to us? Your father and I have been looking for you with great anxiety." And he said to them, "Why were you looking for me? Did you not know that I must be in my Father's house?"

I remember being separated from my mother when I was eight or nine years old. She anxiously searched the store where we were shopping. When she finally found me, I couldn't believe she was upset: "I was only looking at the toys, Mom!"

In this gospel story, Jesus has been lost for several days. He is about twelve years old, and his parents have been searching madly for him, worried and anxious. When they finally find him, Jesus can't believe they are upset: "Didn't you know that I was in my Father's house?"

In writing his gospel, Luke uses the theme of a journey. Less than halfway through his story, Luke tells us that Jesus "set his face toward Jerusalem." The rest of Luke's gospel is the story of that journey. It isn't surprising, then, that at the end of his life, in the final days before his death on the cross, we find Jesus back in Jerusalem – back in "his Father's house." The circle is complete; the journey ends where it began.

When Winter Comes

The circle we see in Luke's gospel calls to mind the circle of our own life. Genesis tells us that "God took the soil of the ground and blew into it the breath of life." The life in us is the "breath of God"; when God "breathes in" again, we die. God draws us back to himself, back to the source of life from which we came, and our body returns to the soil. The circle is complete; the journey ends where it began.

Our loved ones who have died must surely be as mystified by our sorrow as Jesus was when his parents found him in the temple. "Why are you looking for me?" they might ask. "Do you not know that the circle is complete, and the journey ends where it began? Do you not know that God has breathed in again, and I am home? Do you not know that I must be in my Father's house?"

Everything To God In Prayer   Luke 4:38-40

*After he left the synagogue, he entered the house of Simon.
Simon's mother-in-law was afflicted with a severe fever, and
they interceded with him about her. He stood over her,
rebuked the fever, and it left her. She got up immediately and
waited on them.*

*At sunset, all who had people sick with various diseases brought
them to him. He laid his hands on each of them and cured
them.*

My mother went home to the Lord more than seven
years ago. Yet I can still hear her humming those old
Baptist hymns as she worked around the farmhouse: "Oh
what peace we often forfeit / Oh what useless pain we bear
/ All because we do not carry / Everything to God in
prayer."

Mom took everything to God in prayer. As a single parent
struggling to raise seven kids on a broken-down old farm,
without resources and cut off from neighbors by distance
and lack of transportation, she often had nowhere else to
turn.

Mom prayed with expectation – she simply expected God
to do what he had said he would do. It was an oft-repeated
scene at our house: no money, no food, and no way to get
to town to get anything. I was about ten years old, and I
was hungry and crying. Mom put her arm around me and
said, "Don't cry, son. Jesus fed five thousand people –
and there's only eight of us!"

When Winter Comes

James R. Welter

In this gospel passage, the Apostles approach Jesus with expectant faith. Peter's mother-in-law is sick, and they expect Jesus to do something. The gospel reminds us that the healing power of Jesus not only restores us to health, but to active service and care of others: "She got up and began to wait on them."

After the healing, Jesus and the disciples seek a lonely place to rest – but instead, they find another crowd waiting for them! Although weary, Jesus welcomes the people again. He puts the needs of others ahead of everything else. He reminds us that there is no trouble with which he will not assist us, no hardship he will not ease, no bondage from which he will not set us free.

As I write this, I'm very much aware of all those things in my life over which I have no control. All those things I want for those I love. All those things I would do differently. All the time that has gone by and will never return. My soul is hungry, and again I cry.

But I remember the lesson, Mom. I remember the hymn.

The Seventh Chapter:
Running the Race

One of my favorite movies contains the line, "Love isn't going to bed at night – love is getting up in the morning!"

My mother raised seven of us alone on a broken-down farm, without benefit of companionship, transportation, electricity, telephone, or running water. "The long haul" is used these days like it's a new phrase; Mom wrote the book! She spent many, many years being faithful, just "getting up in the morning."

That's the life story of most Christians: there are no thunderbolts to knock us from our horse, no burning bush. There is only the call to live like Christ as we carry out our daily duties – the challenge of faithfully "getting up in the morning."

But if we meet that challenge, we will one day surely hear the words of our Master: "Well done, my good and faithful servant. Well done – and welcome home!"

I'm Still Here   Acts 16:25-28

About midnight, while Paul and Silas were praying and singing hymns to God as the prisoners listened, there was suddenly such a severe earthquake that the foundations of the jail shook; all the doors flew open, and the chains of all were pulled loose. When the jailer woke up and saw the prison doors wide open, he drew [his] sword and was about to kill himself, thinking that the prisoners had escaped. But Paul shouted out in a loud voice, "Do no harm to yourself; we are still here."

Being with people when death has occurred is a privilege; they let you into their lives very quickly and at a deep level. At our parish, we always begin our funeral planning sessions by inviting family members to share their remembrances of the deceased. In those sessions, I often feel as if I'm on holy ground – that I have been trusted to walk where few are invited to go. Frequently, I feel as though *I'm* the one being ministered to, instead of being a minister to someone else.

Carol was middle-aged when she met Bob. But they had only been married a few years when he was diagnosed with cancer, and their remaining thirteen years together were dominated by his battle with that disease. Periodically, Bob would ask, "If you knew it would be like this, would you still have married me?" Her answer was always "Yes." As Bob lay dying, his last words to Carol were, "If you knew it would be like this, would you still have married me?" As he died, she whispered, "Yes."

When Winter Comes
James R. Welter

Paul and Silas did not choose to be in prison; circumstances placed them there. There is an earthquake, their chains are broken, and they have a chance to escape. But they choose to stay because of the harm that would come to their captor if they leave. In the ancient Roman world, a jailer's life was forfeit if his prisoners escaped; Paul's jailer is about to do the honorable thing and "fall on his sword." But at the last moment, he hears those words: "We are still here!" And those words make him open to new life.

Being a Christian is usually not dramatic. Sometimes being a Christian just means saying, "Yes – I'm still here." Is there a part of your life you would like to escape? Maybe it's a troubled marriage, a troublesome job, or a difficult relationship. Maybe you're dealing with sickness, or perhaps it's just the seemingly endless grind of your daily routine. But like Carol, Paul, and Silas, you have instead chosen to say, "Yes, I'm still here!" Those words convey love, give strength, and open us to new life.

"I'm still here!"

Say those words to someone today!

Sow Wheat   Matthew 13:36-39

Then, dismissing the crowds, he went into the house. His disciples approached him and said, "Explain to us the parable of the weeds in the field." He said in reply, "He who sows good seed is the Son of Man, the field is the world, the good seed the children of the kingdom. The weeds are the children of the evil one, and the enemy who sows them is the devil."

By definition, a parable is open-ended; there are no "right" answers about what the parable means. This style of writing seeks to draw the listener into the story: "In your opinion, who was neighbor to the injured man?" *We* write the ending in the answers we give, and in the change it causes in our lives. So when a parable is "explained," we can be very sure that this was not how Jesus originally told the story. Instead, the gospel writer has accommodated the story to his audience, to make sure they got the message he wanted to convey.

There is so much "explaining" in this reflection passage that it's difficult to know what the original point of the story was! But it's pretty clear that Matthew wanted his audience to see that some people had inadvertently let the enemy sow "weeds" in the community. They had allowed themselves to be worn down by pressure and persecution; the faith had never really "taken root" in some of them, while others had been lured away by money and worldly things.

When Winter Comes
James R. Welter

Parables always invite us to apply their lessons to our own life. In the book of Jeremiah, for example, the prophet's first reaction to disaster is to turn inward and recognize that he has "weeds" in his life. He recognizes that he and his people have sinned against the Lord. In the same way, we too are invited to turn inward.

I experience a patient God today, one who allows the weeds and the wheat to grow side by side and allows the rain "to fall on the just and unjust" until the harvest. That patience allows me time to change – it allows me to get control of the "weeds" in my life. It allows me to seek forgiveness, to plant new seeds, and to grow and bear fruit. This parable also warns me that we "reap what we sow." It reminds me that, at harvest time, we will know in which group we belong: the "wheat" or the "chaff."

Others often benefit from the wheat we sow. But we must sow the wheat for our own benefit, too. We must live out of love, not out of what we might want or need from others. I experience this most when someone has injured me. I must forgive them, even if they do not ask for it or recognize that they need forgiveness – even if they think they have done nothing wrong. It is in times like these that I know I must forgive for my *own* sake!

I must do it so the "wheat" in the world can grow. I must do it so *I* can grow, and not let the "weeds" choke the life from who I am. I must do it so that I can bear fruit… and be ready for the harvest.

Whitewashed Tombs   Matthew 23:27-28

Jesus said, "Woe to you, scribes and Pharisees, you hypocrites. You are like whitewashed tombs, which appear beautiful on the outside, but inside are full of dead men's bones and every kind of filth."

"**Y**our issue is one of cognitive dissonance," the counselor said to me one day, as I struggled with my anxiety at being out of the workforce.

Say what?! I had never heard that term before. It sounded like one of those "buzzwords" designed to make people "on the inside" feel smart. I didn't learn until later that it was a term from Psychology 101!

"I'm an accountant," I retorted. "Speak English!"

"Your life is out of balance!" (She caught on quickly!)

"You mean I'm living in two different columns?"

"I mean that your head and your heart are out of sync. Your head says you need a job. Your heart says you need a life! That dissonance – that 'disconnection' – will come out in some way until it is reconciled. That's the tension you feel; that's your stress."

In the time of Jesus, tombs were often placed by the side of the road. They were painted white, which made them glisten in the midday sun, so that people would not accidentally touch them and suffer ritual impurity. Jesus uses that imagery to describe hypocrites, those who pretend to be something they are not. "Woe to you, scribes and Pharisees, you hypocrites!" he says. "For you are like whitewashed tombs, which outwardly appear beautiful, but within are full of dead men's bones and all uncleanness."

That's a pretty vivid metaphor – and it's hard to mistake the meaning!

As Christians, we always struggle against hypocrisy – that "disconnection" between what we say we believe and how we actually live our lives. St. Paul recognized this struggle in his own life: "The good that I would, I do not. The evil I would not – that I do!" It is that "cognitive dissonance" that becomes our growing edge as Christians.

Jesus invites us to love. It is a standing invitation that anticipates a gradually unfolding response. Taken in its entirety, it points to the resolution of the tension between our spontaneous desire for self-rule and the faith invitation to allow our lives to be ruled by God.

If we are to mature in our faith, we must take the time and make an effort to internalize the values we discover in the Gospel. As we grow in the Lord, we will try to lead lives consonant with gospel values, and we will filter out what is dissonant with them. Our "cognitive dissonance" will cease when we identify with the gospel message at the head level, and with the person of Jesus Christ at the heart level.

Then, with St. Augustine, we may "Love and do what you please" – because all that will please us is to respond to the invitation of Jesus to love.

But first, we must align our lives with the gospel message. We must clean out our "whitewashed tombs"!

In what way will you change your life today, so as to live more fully "in sync" with the gospel?

~ Your Reflection ~

When Winter Comes   James R. Welter

~ Your Reflection ~

Hanging In   Genesis 21:14-19

Early the next morning Abraham got some bread and a skin of water and gave them to Hagar. Then, placing the child on her back, he sent her away. As she roamed aimlessly in the wilderness of Beer-sheba, the water in the skin was used up. So she put the child down under a shrub, and then went and sat down opposite him, about a bowshot away; for she said to herself, "Let me not watch to see the child die." As she sat opposite him, he began to cry. God heard the boy's cry, and God's messenger called to Hagar from heaven: "What is the matter, Hagar? Don't be afraid; God has heard the boy's cry in this plight of his. Arise, lift up the boy and hold him by the hand; for I will make of him a great nation." Then God opened her eyes, and she saw a well of water. She went and filled the skin with water, and then let the boy drink.

As my wife and I were raising our two boys, we sometimes remarked, "It's no wonder that God provides *two* parents — it's so each one can get a break once in a while!" I can't imagine anything tougher than being a single parent! My mother raised seven children as a single parent, and my sister Fran raised two. When I once asked Fran how she did it, she replied, "One day at a time. Sometimes one *hour* at a time."

When life is too much to handle and the "big picture" seems too overwhelming, it sometimes helps to break things down into smaller increments. For years, Alcoholics Anonymous has advised participants to approach sobriety "one day at a time."

When Winter Comes
James R. Welter

There is a beautiful line in the movie *Sleepless in Seattle*: Tom Hanks' character is asked how he is dealing with the death of his wife and he replies, "Breathing out and breathing in."

One day at a time. Sometimes one *hour* at a time.

In this story from Genesis, Hagar and her child are cast out into the desert. It is totally unfair and without reason. She weeps as she sees her child lying under the bush, crying out from thirst. So terrible is her sadness and despair that even a strong woman like Hagar must turn away, so that at least she will not have to watch her child die.

What awful hardships and torture they must have suffered in the desert: no food, no water... and no end in sight. Hagar is tough – not just physically, but mentally. That she would even *think* of trying to make it alone in the desert attests to her perseverance. How does she survive? One day at a time. One hour at a time. Breathing out and breathing in... until God reveals the water.

I think that's our message today. Be tough. Survive. Hang in there – one day at a time, one hour at a time...

...until God reveals the water.

Be Fruitful   John 15:8

"By this is my Father glorified, that you bear much fruit and become my disciples."

In my early career, I was in sales. I had a territory and, of course, a quota. One year I landed the proverbial "big order" and was the first person in the office to "make the club." I had my year's quota made by July and I was thrilled. I had succeeded! I reached the epitome of success in sales – I had "produced" my quota! But after a very brief "congratulations," I got the "what-have-you-done-for-me-lately" line. Produce more, my boss told me – go for 200% of quota, be the number one guy in the company! It was at that point that I decided to get out of the sales business.

The command in this short passage from John is to, "Go forth and bear fruit." It echoes the command in Genesis: "Go forth, be fruitful, multiply and fill the earth." These simple phrases speak volumes about the difference between the world and the Gospel! The world would say, "Go forth and be 'productive.'" Make your quota, and then some. But the Gospel says only "be fruitful."

What is the difference between being "fruitful" and being "productive"? Productivity has to do with making things; bearing fruit calls us to "bring forth life." In other words, God doesn't care how many "widgets" (or sales calls) we make – God doesn't give us a quota. God wants us to bring forth *life*. Jesus says, "I have come that you might have life, and have it more abundantly."

When Winter Comes

James R. Welter

There is nothing intrinsically wrong with "production"; the problem in our society is that we define ourselves by what we "produce." In our society, "we are what we make." So everything becomes a "product": house, cars, books, influential friends, successful transactions, important decisions – even goals and ideas. They all become a part of what we have "made." Our ability to produce gives us a sense of being accepted, of being useful, of having value. We even introduce people with emphasis on their productivity: "This is Jim; he made quota, he's in the club, he wrote a book, made mega-millions, etc., etc., etc." We live as if being productive is the same as being "fruitful."

In my life and in my work, am I being fruitful? Is what I do life-giving? Life-sustaining? Am I following God's command to "fill the earth" with the life and love he gave me?

Or am I merely being "productive"?

Take Up Your Mat   John 5:2-9

Now there is in Jerusalem at the Sheep [Gate] a pool called in Hebrew Bethesda, with five porticoes. In these lay a large number of ill, blind, lame, and crippled. One man was there who had been ill for thirty-eight years. When Jesus saw him lying there and knew that he had been ill for a long time, he said to him, "Do you want to be well?" The sick man answered him, "Sir, I have no one to put me into the pool when the water is stirred up; while I am on my way, someone else gets down there before me." Jesus said to him, "Rise, take up your mat, and walk." Immediately the man became well, took up his mat, and walked.

About ten years ago, I dropped out of the corporate world to pursue my Religious Studies degree. It was not an easy decision; I had a long list of reasons why I couldn't do it. I had a long list of "buts": "But I have to work." "But the boys are still in college." "But we need to save for our retirement." My son gave me a book called *Leaving Your Comfort Zone: Let's Get Off Our Buts!* That seems to be the clear message in this passage from John's gospel!

A man has spent thirty-eight years on his back and Jesus asks him, "Do you want to be well?" At first, we might think Jesus is belaboring the obvious, but he seems to know what's going on here. Sure enough, instead of answering with a "yes" or "no," the man has an excuse: "but" no one will help me. Jesus doesn't even acknowledge the excuse – instead, he offers an abrupt challenge: "Rise, take up your mat, and walk."

When Winter Comes

As he nears the end of his life, Jesus is running out of time and patience. This incident doesn't even seem to amount to a cure: Jesus just tells the guy to stop messing around, to stop looking for excuses, to get off his "but"! "Do something!" Jesus seems to say. Start walking! And what happens? The guy walks, for the first time in thirty-eight years, because Jesus said "just DO it."

"Do you *want* to be well?" Jesus asks. If Jesus knows where my heart is, what my desire is, then he also knows my capabilities. He must grow weary of my excuses.

"Do you want to be closer to the Lord? Do you want more time with God?" BUT I am so busy...

"Do you want to care for others?" BUT I have to look out for myself...

"Do you want to feed the hungry, clothe the naked, protect the widow, care for the child?" BUT I'm only one person, and I have a job and a family of my own to worry about...

There is no end to my list of "buts." Yet Jesus knows there is really no good reason why I cannot start walking the walk – right now. The challenge of this passage is clear: "Leave your comfort zone... Get off your 'but'... Do something. Right now!"

Rise, take up your mat... and walk!

Blessed Are You Poor   *Luke 6:20*

And raising his eyes toward his disciples he said:
   "Blessed are you who are poor,
      for the kingdom of God is yours.
   Blessed are you who are now hungry,
      for you will be satisfied."

Anyone who knows me knows that I don't eat chicken. Our boys always found that humorous: they were convinced that it was because, as a child, I once got pecked on the head by a rooster! (I never should have told them that story!) But I'm sure it was because, as a child growing up on the family farm, when we had nothing else left to eat, our last resort was to kill a chicken.

I remember a time we were down to our last chicken – we had only one chicken with which to feed nine people for three days. When I shared that story with a friend, his response was: "Oh, I like chicken salad!" He couldn't conceive of abject poverty: there was no salad, no bread, no salt, no milk – just one chicken. For nine people. For three days.

"Blessed are you poor," Jesus says in Luke's gospel. As a poor, hungry child, I certainly didn't feel blessed. The man who came into my office the other week didn't feel blessed, either: he and his family had been living in a car for several days. Would any of us volunteer for those kinds of "blessings"?

When Winter Comes James R. Welter

So what is Jesus talking about here? How can one possibly find happiness in poverty, hunger, suffering, and sorrow?

Few of us would seek poverty. Nor would a loving God give it to us as some kind of test, or as a means of teaching us a lesson. The fact is that people are poor because we do not respond to the needs of one another. Yet the poor are forced to depend on God – they often have nowhere else to turn. They know that they are not in control of their lives; they know that they cannot "do it themselves." They live in faith, and in their emptiness they turn to the Lord. They come to know that everything is a gift, that all we have is through God's grace. Only when our hands are empty are we open to receive; only when we are hungry can we be fed.

As we sat down to eat our last chicken, my father began to pray: "Bless us, O Lord, and these thy gifts… " My sister and I started to cry. "Why should we pray, when all we have to eat is one puny chicken?" I was only five years old, but I remember the look of surprise on my father's face; it would never have occurred to him to do anything else. "We give thanks to God," he answered, "for whatever we are given."

Blessed are you poor, for yours is the Kingdom of Heaven.

Do Something Radical   Matthew 10:35-38

For I have come to set
*   a man "against his father,*
*   a daughter against her mother,*
*   and a daughter-in-law against her mother-in-law;*
*   and one's enemies will be those of his household."*
Whoever loves father or mother more than me is not worthy
of me, and whoever loves son or daughter more than me is not
worthy of me; and whoever does not take up his cross and
follow after me is not worthy of me.

Reflecting on this passage may make us wonder how Jesus got the title "Prince of Peace"! He sounds like a wild-eyed radical here, someone you might expect to find shouting on a street corner or selling flowers in an airport. This guy's telling us to leave our families, leave our homes, leave our jobs, leave everything that is safe and secure, and follow him! Not only to follow him, but to take up our cross! Take up my cross?! I don't want a cross – I don't even like lumps in my mattress!

In this passage, Jesus is telling us that to follow him, we must make choices. We must put God first. Jesus is also challenging us to give up our mundane lives and superficial security, and to make a commitment to something beyond ourselves. Our need for comfort and security makes it too easy for us to just keep on doing what we've always done, without thinking – and that's not what he wants of us. Jesus makes it clear that he didn't come to justify, defend, or continue the status quo, nor to present us with some kind of easy, "feel-good" religion. He came to shake things up – to cause division, to change lives, to force choices!

We sometimes don't like to think about it, but the Christian life is radical! It puts us at odds with the world. After all, if "all's right with the world," there would be no need for Jesus! But all *isn't* right, and he came to change everything: our comfortable lives, our secure families, our regular jobs, our gated, "safe" communities. He came to change all the things that make us complacent, and to challenge our tolerance of the things that are *wrong* with the world. For if we remain complacent, what will ever change about the world? And if all we ever think about is our own fortunes, our own families, and our own lives and futures, we will never have anything beyond them. We will never have stronger communities. We will never have a more equitable society. We will never have a more honest, more just, more loving world. And we will never have the *true* security, satisfaction, and peace that only a relationship with God can give us.

If we aren't willing to take some risks, make some sacrifices, and shake up our security for Christ, how can we call ourselves his followers? And if we can't be bothered to get up off the couch and do something for our neighbor, how can we call ourselves Christians?

We aren't here to make a living – we're here to make a difference! And Christ didn't come to please or entertain us – he came to change our lives!

Benefit of the Doubt   Matthew 12:8-10

"For the Son of Man is Lord of the sabbath."
Moving on from there, he went into their synagogue. And
behold, there was a man there who had a withered hand.
They questioned him, "Is it lawful to cure on the sabbath?"
so that they might accuse him.

William Proxmire, the one-time Senator from Wisconsin, used to get a lot of publicity (and laughs) by exposing governmental waste: $500 for a hammer, $4 for an aspirin – that sort of thing. His classic case was the government's multi-million-dollar study, at taxpayer expense, to determine why kids fall off bicycles. The study concluded that it's because they "lose their balance"! We all laughed and shook our heads at the stupidity of that study. "C'mon – we all *knew* that!"

But my philosopher son wasn't laughing. He pointed out that we always need to challenge what we think we "know." For thousands of years, he reminded me, everyone assumed that a larger, heavier rock would fall faster than a smaller, lighter one. It was a given – "everyone knew that" – until Galileo dropped two rocks from a tower and disproved what everyone "knew."

We like certainty, being "right," knowing the answers – it gives us the illusion of control over our lives, and makes us feel warm and comfortable. The problem is that, when we "know" something, we aren't open to further learning and growth!

When Winter Comes
James R. Welter

There is a familiar story in the book of Samuel: the prophet Samuel is asked to choose the next king. It's a simple job, because Samuel "knows" the qualifications. But Samuel keeps picking out the wrong person! God has to keep telling him, "Not that one!" Why does Samuel keep making the wrong choice? Because he is looking only at the outside and only in the present! It is God who reads our hearts and sees our potential. So God guides Samuel to the correct choice – the hidden one, the one out tending the sheep – the one who is youngest and most distant, the one *least* likely to be chosen.

In our gospel passage, the Pharisees "know" the law: you don't work on the Sabbath! Everybody "knows" that – it's a given; it's literally the "word of God"! But they are so fixated on what they "know" that they completely miss the *intent* of the law. So when Jesus is about to perform an act of compassion and cure a man's withered hand, the Pharisees object! They miss the meaning of the very law they claim to "know" so well: the Sabbath gives life, so one can and must do what is life-giving on the Sabbath. "So it is lawful to do good on the Sabbath." (v 12)

We like certainty – it makes us feel warm and comfortable. Yet this passage tells us to stop, think, and act carefully. Doubt can be an extraordinary grace! God puts doubt into the mind of Samuel to prevent him from choosing the wrong king. Jesus puts doubt in the minds of the Pharisees to invite them to reinterpret the law and understand more deeply what the Sabbath means.

When we experience doubt as a means to greater insight, rather than as a threat, it can be a positive influence. When we doubt our first impressions, we may take the time to look more closely and learn something new. When we doubt what is on the surface, we may see people differently. When we doubt what we "know," it opens our hearts to new knowledge and experiences. When we doubt our own motivations and the "rightness" of our actions, we may change how we act toward others.

Let's give ourselves – and each other – the "benefit of the doubt" today!

~ Your Reflection ~

When Winter Comes

James R. Welter

~ Your Reflection ~

The Eighth Chapter:
Called to Serve

Jesus did not choose "superstars" as his first followers; there were no former class valedictorians or company presidents in their number! Jesus chose very ordinary people. They were non-professionals who had no wealth or position, chosen from among common people who did everyday things. Jesus chose these people not for what they were, but for what they were capable of becoming.

God still chooses ordinary people. So, when the Lord calls us to serve, we must not hold back because we think that we have little to offer. And we must never consider ourselves, or anyone else, insignificant. We are mustard seed. We are yeast.

God chooses us not for what we are, but for what we can become!

Come With Me
Into The Fields

Matthew 9:36-38

At the sight of the crowds, his heart was moved with pity for them because they were troubled and abandoned, like sheep without a shepherd. Then he said to his disciples, "The harvest is abundant but the laborers are few; so ask the master of the harvest to send out laborers for his harvest."

The last board of our new home (it was new thirty years ago!) was hardly in place when my wife announced, "And I want a garden right there." I couldn't believe my ears. "A garden? Why would you want a garden?" Childhood memories flooded my mind; a garden was a lot of work, a means of survival. "Hoe the garden" was the rural Indiana equivalent of "clean your room" – it was the ultimate punishment for a kid! "Cincinnati isn't that far; my Dad will come and help me take care of it," my wife assured me. "You won't have to do a thing." (Oh, sure – I believe that…!)

But every spring for ten years, my wife's father came in from Cincinnati with his load of "out-of-state manure." "Doesn't that stuff come in bags now?" I mumbled from the comfort of my patio chair as I watched the garden become bigger and bigger. It took over much of our backyard. "Uh… you can't plow a patio, can you, honey?" I asked, seeking assurance that farming techniques hadn't progressed further than I thought!

This gospel passage inspired one of my favorite hymns, which includes the line: "The harvest is plenty / the

James R. Welter

laborers are few / come with me into the fields." From life on the farm as I child, I can certainly tell all you "city slickers" why the "laborers are few": fieldwork is back-breaking labor! From planting corn to baling hay, the work is endless – there is always more to do, and success is not guaranteed. You don't know when the rains will come; often the fruits of your labor must wait until "next year" when conditions are better. And of course, the "laborers" don't own the farm; it's not their corn or their fruit. Some unknown, unseen person will benefit in some unknown future time. It takes great faith to farm.

"Come to the garden!" was the childhood cry of the vanquished one who had suffered that "ultimate punishment" and been sent out to hoe. Brothers and sisters responded, rivalries were forgotten – soon the workers were two, then three, then four or five. Our work became play: "I'll bet I can weed faster than you can hoe…!" It was my sister Fran again, standing at the head of an onion row. We all knew – the entire 4-H Club knew! – that Fran had no equal in weeding onions.

As children, the difference between work and play was of-ten the invitation – and the attitude. "Come with me into the fields" is God's invitation. You will not be alone; you will have each other, and I will be with you. I will turn your labor into joy. Trust me to send the rain, and believe me when I say, "The harvest is plenty."

Come with me into the fields!

We Are Called   Matthew 10:2-4

The names of the twelve apostles are these: first, Simon called Peter, and his brother Andrew; James, the son of Zebedee, and his brother John; Philip and Bartholomew, Thomas and Matthew the tax collector; James, the son of Alphaeus, and Thaddeus; Simon the Cananean, and Judas Iscariot who betrayed him.

It is clear in this gospel passage that Jesus chooses very ordinary people to bring about the kingdom. Look at the twelve who were chosen: they were not professionals; they had no wealth or position. They were chosen from among common people who did ordinary things – they had no special education, no social advantages.

It gets worse! He chooses those who would deny him. I deny Jesus every time I choose a false god – wealth, power, fame, or popularity. I deny Jesus when I allow my job, or my need for security or possessions, to be first in my life. He chooses those who deny him, like Simon Peter... like me.

He chooses the zealots, those who resort to violence to deal with problems. I often respond "in kind" when I'm treated unfairly. Sometimes my actions hurt my family, my neighbor, or my co-workers. He chooses those who resort to violence, like Judas... like me.

He chooses ambitious people, those who look out for number one. I have angled for the biggest desk, the corner office with the view; I have fought for promotions, raises, and titles. I have put my job before my family, or slighted a colleague for my own advantage. He chooses ambitious people like the Sons of Zebedee... like me.

He chooses the tax collectors, those that take advantage of the less fortunate. I often buy the cheapest item, without regard for the unjust labor that brought it to me. Sometimes I agree to be "paid in cash" to avoid my share of the tax, or I "forget" to fill in that line on the form that would send more of my money to fund programs for the poor. He chooses tax collectors like Matthew... like me.

He chooses those who doubt. I have the need to take control, to be in charge and "make things happen." In my desperate self-reliance, I doubt that God is aware of my needs or will take care of them; I doubt that he will help me. He chooses those who doubt, like Thomas... like me.

God sends out imperfect, ordinary people to proclaim the presence of his kingdom and to heal those who are suffering. Obviously, God doesn't choose us because we are denying, violent, ambitious, greedy, or doubting! Perhaps instead God sees in us what we oftentimes do not: our courage, our faithfulness, our enthusiasm, our persistence, our sincerity... our willingness to keep on trying.

God does not choose us for what we are – God chooses us for what we are capable of becoming.

What is God calling you to "become" today?

A Big Church On Michigan Road   Luke 10:29

But because he wished to justify himself, he said to Jesus, "And who is my neighbor?"

"There are two guys out there who are asking for assistance," my secretary informs me. "Well, I'm way over budget," I respond. "I'll just go out and tell them we don't have any money left and we can't help."

The walk across the office becomes for me a journey in time...

... suddenly, it's 1950. I am ten years old. I am standing with my big brother in the barn of our neighbor – my God-father, my father's friend. We see him often, passing our house on his way to church, passing our house returning from town, flying his plane overhead. "We don't have anything to eat," I hear my brother report. "Could we have $15.00 for groceries? We can pay you back when our welfare check comes." I am ten. I don't understand the answer: "Get out of the barn – you're scaring the cows." We are standing outside now. "What does that mean?" I asked my brother. "It means we go back home. We'll have to think of something else."

I am ten. I cry.

"We can't help everyone – the funds just aren't there," I think to myself as I meet the two men. The least I can do is treat them with dignity: "Come on back to my office, guys, and have a seat. How did you happen to come to us?" "We asked some lady to help us, and she said there was a big church on Michigan Road," the older man says. "She didn't know the name of it, but she suggested we come here for help." It strikes me that our building's visibility from the street brings many to us. It interrupts our day and taxes our funds. And deciding if the need is real and how we can best help always causes stress. "We are stranded," the younger man continues. "We slept in our car. We need to stay overnight to have the car fixed, we need gas, and we're hungry." Maybe it's the fact that they are from a place near my hometown that strikes a chord with me. Maybe it's the rate at which they consume the jellybeans from the candy jar on my desk that convinces me their hunger is real.

"All day yesterday we begged, but no one would help us," he went on. "People kept asking us to leave." "Nice neighbors," I mumbled. "Maybe you were scaring the cows!"

A quick phone call and a night's lodging is arranged. A food voucher and a tank of gas bring smiles, and greasy, smelly hugs all around. "You're doing all of this for us? This really is a 'big' church!"

The good and generous people of St. Monica Parish have allowed me to be a "neighbor" in their name. They have allowed me to be the presence of Christ to these men. It feels good to be able to give.

I am sixty. Again I cry.

Let The Dead Bury The Dead

Matthew 8:19-22

A scribe approached and said to him, "Teacher, I will follow you wherever you go." Jesus answered him, "Foxes have dens and birds of the sky have nests, but the Son of Man has nowhere to rest his head." Another of [his] disciples said to him, "Lord, let me go first and bury my father." But Jesus answered him, "Follow me, and let the dead bury their dead."

Once again it is helpful to us, when we read scripture, to consider the culture and times in which it was written. In this passage, a man asks to be allowed to bury his father before he follows Jesus – and Jesus says, "No way! Let the dead bury the dead."

What?! Is Jesus saying that this guy can't even go to his own father's funeral?

No, the man just meant that he had responsibilities at home. He wanted to go back home and take care of his father until his father died; it didn't necessarily mean that his father was dead or near death. There were no social security payments or 401K retirement plans in the time of Jesus, so children were expected to take care of their aging parents. Jesus was appealing to the man's heart and telling him to detach himself from whatever might hold him back, whatever might prevent him from following. Jesus was also indicating that the way would not be easy – that sacrifices would have to be made.

When Winter Comes James R. Welter

Before we "sign on" for something, it is quite natural to ask what it will cost us. In other words, what's the level of our commitment? Are we willing to make sacrifices? Jesus made sure that any would-be followers knew what they were getting into – indeed, he warned this one: before you follow me, think what you are doing and count the cost. A disciple must be willing to make sacrifices – even to sacrifice his own life. Following Jesus isn't a walk in the park – it's the narrow road, the "road less traveled." And it's that way for a reason: it's uphill, it's difficult, people throw rocks at you, and if you follow too closely, they might even kill you!

I often feel that Christian life ought to be easier. If I'm trying to do the right thing, why should it be so hard? Why do I get beat up for my efforts? We always expect the arrow to hit the other guy; we are surprised when bad things happen to us. "Not in this family," we think. "Not in our neighborhood!"

In his gospel and in the book of Acts, Luke shatters our illusions of an easy road. In his gospel, he traces the journey of Jesus to Jerusalem... and his death. In Acts, he traces the journey of Paul to Rome... and his death. Luke invites us to walk the journey – but be warned, he tells us! This is what happened to Jesus; this is what happened to Paul. If you accept this invitation... guess what may happen to you!

But we can still walk the journey... because we know that we do not walk alone. We know who walks with us!

Travel Light   Luke 9:1-3

He summoned the Twelve and gave them power and au-
thority over all demons and to cure diseases, and he sent
them to proclaim the kingdom of God and to heal [the
sick]. He said to them, "Take nothing for the journey,
neither walking stick, nor sack, nor food, nor money, and
let no one take a second tunic."

The type of person I like to see on a committee are those
who prevent "group-think" – the free-thinkers who have a
knack for "cutting to the chase." They usually have little
patience for studies, bylaws, action plans, or subcommit-
tees; their approach is usually simple and direct. I think I'd
let Jesus serve on my committee (although I'm not sure
he'd take the job!), because he has a way of simplifying things.
Ten Commandments? You can cover them in two: love
God and love your neighbor. Tax problem? Give to
Caesar what is Caesar's. Who is your neighbor? Whoever
is in need. It's not complicated – so get on with it!

The directions Jesus gives to the disciples in this passage are
simple, direct, and reflective of common sense. He shows
no need to control or "micro-manage" – he just wants the
job done. He's clear about the task ahead and advises how
to steer around distractions or difficulties. "Provide
yourselves with neither gold nor silver nor copper in your
belts; no traveling bag, no change of shirt, no sandals, no
walking staff." In other words, travel light. Forget about
the non-essentials and leave behind anything that will
distract you from your mission.

When Winter Comes
James R. Welter

One of Stephen Covey's *Seven Habits of Effective People* is to "begin with the end in mind." It's not a bad principle for Christian living: where do you want to be at the "end"? What will be needed to get you there? And what extras, what distractions, what baggage do you need to leave behind? A defining question might be, "Will this help me to reach my goal?" In military jargon, is it "mission-essential"? Will it help get me to the "end" I have in mind? And if not, I must let go of it – it has to be left behind!

Are you willing to travel light? Are you ready to leave behind those things that will hinder you in your mission to live the Gospel message? Are you willing to leave behind your anger? Your resentments? Your destructive relationships? Your pride? Your jealousy? Your selfishness? Your "gold"?

It's not complicated – so get on with it!

Jesus Knocking   Revelation 3:20

"Behold, I stand at the door and knock. If anyone hears my voice and opens the door, then I will enter his house and dine with him, and he with me."

Most of us are familiar with the famous painting of Jesus standing at the door knocking; it was inspired by this passage from the book of Revelation: "Behold, I stand at the door and knock." Less obvious is how the artist captures the second line of the passage: "If anyone hears my voice and opens the door…" In the painting, there is no handle visible on the door – because the door must be opened from the inside. *We* must open the door, as scripture says. We must open the "door" of our heart before Jesus can enter.

Jesus does not use force; he doesn't kick the door down. He invites: "I stand at the door and knock." If we do not answer the door, nothing will happen! It's indicative of how much control we have over our own world and our own destiny. It shows how much God depends on *us* to bring about his kingdom. This may not seem like a very efficient way to run a world, but it's God's way! Perhaps that's because efficiency isn't the goal – rather, God's goal is to establish a relationship with us.

So Jesus doesn't come through the door by force, like a burglar might – instead, he knocks, and we answer. He invites, and we respond. He loves, and we love in return. And the kingdom grows.

When Winter Comes

James R. Welter

Jesus doesn't use force, but that is not to say he isn't persistent! In a sense, Jesus is *always* "knocking at our door." He is always inviting us. Jesus first invites us to "awareness" – he invites us to an awareness of God in us, and what it means to be the Beloved. He invites us to an awareness of our gifts, and to an awareness of who we are at the core of our being. Out of that "BE"-ing, he invites us to "DO"-ing: to serving, healing, forgiving, feeding, and loving.

Am I ready to open my door, so that Jesus may more fully enter my life?

I hear you Lord – knocking at my door. Why do I hesitate? Why do I not run to you?

I hear you Lord – knocking at my door. Why do I fear?

I hear you Lord – knocking at my door. What is it you ask of me? What is it you offer me? To come? To follow? To belong? To leave all? To let go? To be free?

You ask me to believe. You invite me to trust. You offer me hope. You give me love.

I hear you Lord – knocking at my door.

Loopholes   Luke 10:25-29

There was a scholar of the law who stood up to test him and said, "Teacher, what must I do to inherit eternal life?" Jesus said to him, "What is written in the law? How do you read it?" He said in reply, "You shall love the Lord, your God, with all your heart, with all your being, with all your strength, and with all your mind, and your neighbor as yourself." He replied to him, "You have answered correctly; do this and you will live." But because he wished to justify himself, he said to Jesus, "And who is my neighbor?"

"**M**y sister called – a friend of hers is stranded downtown," my wife said to me one morning. "Will you please stop at the bus station and loan him some money?" "But honey, I've just started a new job," I protested. "I don't want to be late getting to the office." "Remember, dear," she reminded me, "the Good Samaritan was on his way somewhere else, too." She was right; I had been looking for an easy way out – a loophole, an excuse – some justification for not having to play that role. On my way to work, I stopped by and loaned him the money.

In this gospel passage, "a scholar of the law" wants to know how narrowly Jesus defines the criteria for "who counts" as a neighbor (and who can be excluded). He seems to be looking for a limitation on his obligation to love and care for others, a way out – a loophole. And (as any modern lawyer will also tell you) defining terms is a good way to find loopholes, so he asks Jesus, "Who is my neighbor?"

When Winter Comes

James R. Welter

During my visit to the Holy Land in 1995, I stood on the road from Jerusalem to Jericho. It still exists, and it is a timeless scene (the desert doesn't change much). It was a place where one could really get a sense of what things were like in the time of Jesus. Back then, the road from Jerusalem to Jericho was desolate and dangerous, and was notorious for its robbers – no one in their right mind would travel that road alone.

In the parable that Jesus told (v 30-35), the priest who passed by the fallen traveler found a loophole: he was on his way to worship and didn't want to risk the possibility of ritual impurity by touching that dirty, bleeding man. No doubt he said a prayer for all those injured and laying on the side of the road as he continued his journey. His piety got in the way of his charity. The Levite who later came along approached close to the victim, but stopped short of actually helping him. He too found a loophole: the bandits might be waiting to ambush him. Perhaps the Levite, a temple functionary, made a mental note to propose that a committee be formed to study the problem of crime on the roadways. He put his personal safety ahead of saving his neighbor, and traveled on.

And today, we, too, have our favorite loopholes: she shouldn't have been dressed that way; they should budget their money better; he could get a job if he really wanted one; those kind of people are just no good; it's not my job; there's nothing *I* can do about it; no one in their right mind would travel that road alone.

By telling the parable of the Good Samaritan, Jesus closes each of our loopholes. He tells us that we must be willing to help, even if the "victims" brought trouble upon themselves – even if it was "their own fault." He tells us that our love and desire to help others must be practical, that "good intentions" are not enough. He tells us that we must help those in need, even if it is inconvenient or takes us out of our way. He tells us that we must love as God loves – unconditionally, excluding no one. And he tells us that no excuse for doing otherwise is acceptable.

Although we are the Samaritan, we are also the Innkeeper – for it is to us that Jesus brings the poor, the injured, the weak, the disadvantaged, and the downtrodden.

It is to us that he says, "Take care of them until my return!"

What will you do to care for them today?

James R. Welter

~ Your Reflection ~

Our Guest List   Luke 14:12-14

Then he said to the host who invited him, "When you hold a lunch or a dinner, do not invite your friends or your brothers or your relatives or your wealthy neighbors, in case they may invite you back and you have repayment. Rather, when you hold a banquet, invite the poor, the crippled, the lame, the blind; blessed indeed will you be because of their inability to repay you. For you will be repaid at the resurrection of the righteous."

There are many stories in the gospels of Jesus at someone's table. He attended so many feasts and parties that he was even accused of being "a drunkard and a glutton"! As far as we can tell from the gospel accounts, Jesus never refused a dinner invitation – although I doubt he got invited back very often! In this passage, he again goes to dinner and lectures his host, this time about who the host should and shouldn't invite! He's been invited to a party, and he's criticizing the guest list!

"So why did you invite these people to your party? Is it because they will invite you to theirs? So you show favor and generosity to those who will repay you in kind… but what about those who don't have the means to repay you – the poor, the sick, and the disadvantaged? Why do you not invite them? By the way, why did you invite me? Did you expect some favor or reward? Maybe a little healing, a 'sign' or two on the side? Did you want to impress your neighbors by hosting the famous 'miracle worker' from Galilee?"

169

When Winter Comes

(I imagine the disciples were pretty embarrassed: "Oh boy – here he goes, harassing the host again!" "Yeah – it'll take a 'miracle' to get us invited back, that's for sure!")

Jesus likes to probe our hearts. He wants us to be honest with ourselves, and he challenges us to examine the motivations for our actions. How would Jesus feel about your "guest list"? How would he feel about the kind of people you invite into your life? In what ways do you invite the poor, the sick, the disadvantaged, to your "party"? Can you call by name the person who cleans the restroom or empties the trashcans at your place of work (or worship)? What about the homeless person who asks you for help on the street? Do you ask about their family, or listen to their hopes and dreams? Do you give to others as freely as Jesus gave, without expectation of personal gain or reward? Or do you expect repayment?

God invites us to his table – we, who cannot repay. He hosts the feast; he provides the meal. Ours is merely to share his bounty with others. *We* must invite the guests.

Who will you invite today?

The Rich Man and Lazarus   Luke 16:19-23

There was a rich man who dressed in purple garments and fine linen and dined sumptuously each day. And lying at his door was a poor man named Lazarus, covered with sores, who would gladly have eaten his fill of the scraps that fell from the rich man's table. Dogs even used to come and lick his sores. When the poor man died, he was carried away by angels to the bosom of Abraham. The rich man also died and was buried, and from the netherworld, where he was in torment, he raised his eyes and saw Abraham far off and Lazarus at his side.

My wife, Helen, has worked with the terminally ill as a hospice nurse for more than fifteen years. She has comforted more than two thousand people as they passed from this life. She has held the hand of many as they breathed their last. Helen has never witnessed a deathbed conversion, and her explanation for this is simple: "People die the way they live." Even at the point of death, their attitude about life doesn't change.

There is no indication that the rich man in this gospel passage is a particularly bad person. We are not told that he got his money dishonestly or that he was a notorious sinner. But he does enjoy his luxury, and doesn't care about the poor beggar at his gate. Even when he's dead, his attitude doesn't change: he still sees Lazarus as "beneath" him, and tries to order him about as if he were a slave. "Tell Lazarus to get me some water," he demands. "Send Lazarus back to see my brothers…" That will

scare the "hell" out of them, and they'll change their attitude and their lives. But even as he speaks, the rich man
himself – with his own arrogant, unfeeling attitude – is
undying proof that they will not.

Parables are intended to get us to identify with the characters, so names are generally not used. This parable is the
only exception in the New Testament: the character
"Lazarus" is named, seemingly alluding to the "Lazarus"
whom Jesus raised from the dead. Using that name for
the character underscores the point that "even though
someone be raised from the dead, they will not believe"…
and they won't change their attitude – or their lives.

Although this parable clearly hints at the Resurrection, it
really isn't about miracles, because (as the story points out)
people aren't converted by miracles. People aren't converted
by testimony, either… even if it comes from one who has
risen from the dead. People are converted only when they
open their hearts and lives to God. And the only way to get
people to do that is to open *our* hearts and *our* lives to them,
and let God work through us.

This parable isn't about miracles… it's about our attitude
toward others. It's about looking at our neighbor, and acknowledging his or her needs. It's about learning to open
our "gates" to others, and helping others to open theirs.
This parable is about sharing our wealth. This parable is
about sharing God's love.

This parable is about what it means to be a Christian!

You Feed Them! Mark 6:35-37

By now it was already late and his disciples approached him and said, "This is a deserted place and it is already very late. Dismiss them so that they can go to the surrounding farms and villages and buy themselves something to eat." He said to them in reply, "You give them something to eat."

One of my all-time favorite movies is *Oh God!*, with George Burns and John Denver. God (Burns) comes to earth in modern times and appears to the manager of a grocery store (Denver). In one of many profound and challenging scenes (amidst the comedy), Denver complains to God, "It's so hard for us down here – why don't you give us some help?!" And God replies, "I gave you each other."

So often we want God to make our lives easy; we want him to do things *for* us. Yet God has already given us everything we need: our talents, our capabilities, our intelligence and resourcefulness – and, of course, each other. But instead of using what he has given us, we constantly ask him to make an exception – to break the natural laws he has created and "give us a miracle"!

The multiplication of the loaves is the only miracle story common to all four gospels. Gospels have been defined as "theology in narrative form," so it isn't surprising that each writer emphasizes a different aspect of the story, according to his audience and the lesson each writer wants to teach. There is an interesting line in Mark's rendition, for example, that leads some scholars to conclude that the "miracle of the loaves" was considerably different from our traditional understanding. Like us, the Apostles go to Jesus with a problem and expect a quick, easy answer. The crowd is hungry – there are thousands of them, they are far from home, and it would take six months' wages to buy enough bread to feed them all. Clearly, "this is a job for Jesus" – we need a miracle! Yet Jesus replies, "You give them something to eat." In some translations, the reply is even more direct: "*You* feed them!" In other words, don't expect me to break the natural laws and just "whip you up" a miracle for your convenience – God has already given you everything you need. So *you* feed them!

When the first person comes forth with what he has – "a few loaves and some fish" – Jesus looks up to heaven and blesses it. Perhaps he was praying for God to encourage generous hearts. And perhaps others then began bringing out what they had (it's unlikely that, in a crowd of five thousand people far from home, only one thought to bring a lunch!). Then, with all present sharing what they have with one another, "it's a miracle" – there's enough for everyone! And truly, which is the greater marvel: manufacturing some extra food, or transforming five thousand stingy, self-centered people into ones who care and share freely with each other?

In the end, it isn't bread and fish that Jesus wants to change. It's *us*.

When Did We See You   Matthew 25:42-44
Hungry?

"For I was hungry and you gave me no food, I was thirsty and you gave me no drink, a stranger and you gave me no welcome, naked and you gave me no clothing, ill and in prison, and you did not care for me." Then they will answer and say, 'Lord, when did we see you hungry or thirsty or a stranger or naked or ill or in prison, and not minister to your needs?'"

It gets very tiring. I answer the phone and the telemarketer on the other end asks, "Is your husband at home?" There is little evidence of Christian patience or charity in my voice when I reply, "I *am* the husband!"

"Do you want to see God?" my younger brother's deep, professionally-trained voice (which was surely intended for me, the older brother) booms to the students in his Confirmation class. "Do you want to see Christ? Then look at the person next to you. If you don't see Christ there, then you will never see him."

Matthew's judgment scene makes the same point.

I was hungry, and you asked me to wait.

I was hungry, and you formed a committee.

I was hungry, and you built a corporate headquarters.

When Winter Comes
James R. Welter

I was hungry, and you said, "they're foreigners."

I was hungry, and you said, "there will always be poor people."

I was hungry, and you said, "they're lazy and don't want to work."

I was hungry, and you said, "we don't hire anyone over 45 years old."

I was hungry, and you said, "profits are down; we have to let you go."

I was hungry, and instead of educating children, you armed a soldier.

I was hungry, and instead of buying medicine, you built a jet fighter.

I was hungry, and instead of building houses, you bombed another country.

Lord, when did we see you hungry?

No 'Plan B'   Matthew 5:13
"You are the salt of the earth."

Jesus used many ordinary images, such as salt, to convey extraordinary truths. Salt was a valuable commodity in the ancient world, and it served a very useful purpose in hot climates before the invention of electricity and refrigeration. Salt not only gave flavor to food – it also prevented meat from spoiling. Jesus uses the image of salt to describe how his disciples are to live in the world: as salt penetrates, purifies, and preserves food, so Christians must be "salt" – to penetrate, purify, and preserve our world with God's Word.

When discussions turn to how God's will interacts with our will, one of my favorite sayings is, "God always has a 'Plan B'." By this, I mean that, although we have free will, God always has a way to get his will accomplished. God will go to "Plan B" to get his will done, based on whatever choices we make.

So it got my attention the other day when I heard a preacher say, "God has no 'Plan B'!" He went on: "God only has 'Plan A'... and you're it!" He was speaking in a different context than that in which I normally use the term, but his message was certainly powerful: God only has 'Plan A'... and *you're it!*

God's work only gets done by us – by those who are the "salt of the earth." It gets done by those who give flavor to life. It gets done when we penetrate the darkness of our world with the light of Christ. It gets done when we purify ourselves and preserve the gospel message by the way we live our lives. God's work gets done by those who strengthen and season life with love, mercy, forgiveness, tenderness, compassion, and comfort.

God has no "Plan B." God only has "Plan A"... and you're it!

~ Your Reflection ~

The Ninth Chapter:
Emmanuel – God With Us

For me, the most powerful words in scripture are in a name. Emmanuel – "God with us." When we are in perplexing circumstances and facing insurmountable problems, these words assure us that we are not alone – God is with us!

I identify with Joseph in the Christmas story, because I'm so often clueless as to what's really going on in my life. Not all of us have angels communicating to us in dreams! But we can all feel the movements of God's spirit in our own lives. Maybe that's the point of the Advent and Christmas stories: to remind us that "God is with us."

The point of the Christmas story isn't the star's guiding light. The point of the story isn't the wise men bearing gifts, nor the poverty of a couple giving birth in a stable. It is in the words of an angel, the words that reveal to us the meaning of the child's name – "God is with us."

If we live our lives in the light of that name, if we seek that light though our joys and sorrows, if we believe – *and live as if we believe* – that "God is with us," then we also take part in the Christmas story. We take part in the ongoing "birth" of Jesus in our world.

Voice In the Desert   John 1:19-23

And this is the testimony of John. When the Jews from Jerusalem sent priests and Levites [to him] to ask him, "Who are you?" he admitted and did not deny it, but admitted, "I am not the Messiah." So they asked him, "What are you then? Are you Elijah?" And he said, "I am not." "Are you the Prophet?" He answered, "No." So they said to him, "Who are you, so we can give an answer to those who sent us? What do you have to say for yourself?" He said:

"I am 'the voice of one crying out in the desert,
"Make straight the way of the Lord,'"
as Isaiah the prophet said."

"**W**ho are you?" In this passage from St. John's gospel, John the Baptist has no difficulty answering that question when the authorities come to investigate him. The Jewish leaders sincerely wanted to know if the Messiah had come, so they sent priests to ask if John claimed to be the Messiah or one of the great prophets who was expected to return (see Malachi 4:5, Deuteronomy 18:15).

John has no identity crisis. He knows who he is. Actually, John knows two things: he knows that he is *not* the Messiah, and he knows that Jesus *is* the Messiah! Those of us who try to see our world with the eyes of faith hopefully take advantage of the seasons of Advent and Christmas to restore ourselves in Christ, and arrive at the beginning of the new year filled and renewed with God's spirit. At that point, we, too, know that *we* are not the Messiah, and that Jesus is the Messiah! As the year progresses, however, I know I'll soon have difficulty remembering what John knew so well: "I am not the Messiah!" I'll begin to forget – once again! – that I'm not infallible, that I don't control things, and that I don't have all the answers. As Oscar Romero put it: "We are workers, not master builders; ministers, not Messiahs. We are prophets of a future not our own."

The Church seems to recognize how quickly the resolve we have during Advent and Christmas is challenged. Mindful of what we face in our everyday world, many of the Lectionary readings at the first of the new year center around problems experienced by the early Church. The then-new Christian communities quickly encountered false teachers and people who dismissed Christ's divinity and oneness with the Father. We, too, face the distractions of our less-than-perfect world when we return to our everyday lives and routines after the holidays. We must move quickly from our celebration of the arrival of Jesus back to our life beyond his coming. All too soon, it's back to the "dungeon," back to the "rat race," back to the "desert"! Back to being the "lone voice" crying out: "Stop this hatred! Stop this killing! Stop this war! Stop this injustice! Come into the light! Christ has come. Hope has come. Salvation has come. The Light shines, even amidst the darkness. Jesus lives!"

How will you announce his presence today?

Genealogy   *Matthew 1:1-2*

The book of the genealogy of Jesus Christ, the son of David, the son of Abraham.

Abraham became the father of Isaac, Isaac the father of Jacob, Jacob the father of Judah and his brothers.

Matthew begins his gospel with a genealogy, a list of ancestral names. It goes on and on for seventeen verses and reminds me of the punch line to an old joke about the telephone book: "Not much of a plot, but it sure has a cast of characters!"

Genealogies in scripture serve several purposes: they make a connection with the past, establish the authenticity of the last person in the line, and often serve as a literary device which connects the stories. But there are sometimes other, more subtle messages imbedded in what seems like an endless recitation of names. Matthew traces the genealogy of Jesus back to Abraham, while Luke (3:23-38) traces Jesus all the way back to Adam. The reason for this difference is found in the intent of each author and the message each wants to convey to his readers. Matthew wants to root Jesus in the heritage of Israel and identify him as the Messiah who is to come from the line of David. Luke presents Jesus as a universal savior, and so traces his heritage all the way back to the "universal ancestor," Adam.

In a patriarchal society such as that of the ancient Hebrews, it isn't surprising for Matthew to trace the lineage of Jesus through his male ancestry. Thus, Matthew begins his list with Abraham (founder of the Hebrew nation), moves through the high point of Israel's history with King David, hits the low point during the Babylonian exile, and ends with its fulfillment in Jesus, the Messiah.

But this all-male genealogy is broken by the inclusion of four "unusual" (and questionable) women: Tamar conceived her sons by her father-in-law; Rahab was a prostitute; Ruth, a Moabite, deserted her tribe; and Bathsheba married King David after he arranged the death of her first husband! It isn't by accident that the infancy narrative of Jesus immediately follows Matthew's genealogy – by including those surprising names (and events) in his genealogy of the Messiah, Matthew seems to be preparing us for the "unusual" way in which God enters our world through the birth of Jesus.

He also seems to be telling us that God doesn't always work in the manner we expect. God's blessings often come into our lives in the most unusual and unexpected ways, and through the most unlikely people (sometimes in spite of those people's failings, weaknesses, and sins). So a homeless wanderer becomes the father of a nation, a young shepherd boy becomes the King of Israel... and the baby born in a manger becomes the Messiah and Savior.

To touch our hearts, God often uses the last person we would expect. And to touch the hearts of others, he also uses the last person we would expect – us!

How will you allow God to use *you* this Advent season?

Your Plan Follows Us   Luke 1:30-37

Then the angel said to her, "Do not be afraid, Mary, for you have found favor with God. Behold, you will conceive in your womb and bear a son, and you shall name him Jesus. He will be great and will be called Son of the Most High, and the Lord God will give him the throne of David his father, and he will rule over the house of Jacob forever, and of his kingdom there will be no end." But Mary said to the angel, "How can this be, since I have no relations with a man?" And the angel said to her in reply, "The holy Spirit will come upon you, and the power of the Most High will overshadow you. Therefore the child to be born will be called holy, the Son of God. And behold, Elizabeth, your relative, has also conceived a son in her old age, and this is the sixth month for her who was called barren; for nothing will be impossible for God."

I'm not going to admit my age, but I find myself identifying with Elizabeth and Zechariah rather than with Mary and Joseph this Advent season. Did you notice that, when Mary questioned the angel in this passage, she was consoled and given assurance – but in the preceding passages, when Zechariah asked a question ("How am I to know this?"), he was struck dumb? (Lk 1:18-20)

OK, bad choice of words for Zack – you never want to tick off an angel! But who could blame him for doubting? Mary is young (scholars think she was about 15 years old), and God hasn't asked much of her yet. She's excited: a new baby, a special calling from God – she can't wait to tell her cousin!

When Winter Comes

On the other hand, Zechariah was called by God years ago and now he's retired. He's "been there, done that"; he has paid his dues.

Scripture tells us that Elizabeth and Zechariah are "righteous in the eyes of God, observing all the commandments and ordinances of the Lord blamelessly." They have spent their lives saying "yes" to God. They have also spent years praying for a child, but Elizabeth was barren and everyone knew it. The once-young couple was now old, and the long wait had become resignation. Sadness creased their faces, as years passed and they accepted their situation. They could see the emptiness in each other's eyes. They have made adjustments and finally accepted what cannot be changed: they will grow old alone.

Now the angel speaks: Listen! God has a message for you. No wonder Zechariah has a question! Listen? Didn't we already answer your call? Didn't we accept our fate? Haven't we paid our dues? But the angel says: God doesn't want you to "accept" – he wants you to *listen!* Listen again, as in your youth. Listen with excitement, with anticipation, without doubting. It is easier for you to "accept" than to listen – because listening to God requires change, a new direction; listening to God requires you to redefine yourself – again. Despite your age, despite your previous faith, you haven't yet heard *this* message! You haven't "been there, done that!" You haven't yet been where I'm going to take you; you haven't yet done what I'm going to ask of you.

Give us ears to hear you, O Lord, because our sight fails us and we cannot see where you will take us. Remind us again: your plan doesn't call for mere acceptance, and your plan doesn't call for surrender. Your plan calls for an eager spirit, an open mind, and an attentive heart. Your plan follows us into darkness; your plan accompanies us into barrenness. Your plan follows us to places we think you do not dwell. Like dreams of our youth, you call us still.

Like dreams of our youth – you call us still.

How will you answer God's call today?

~ Your Reflection ~

When Winter Comes

James R. Welter

~ Your Reflection ~

The Light Shines   John 1:1-5

In the beginning was the Word,
*   and the Word was with God,*
*   and the Word was God.*
He was in the beginning with God.
All things came to be through him,
*   and without him nothing came to be.*
What came to be through him was life,
*   and this life was the light of the human race;*
the light shines in the darkness,
*   and the darkness has not overcome it.*

In the pre-Vatican world, this reading was read as the "last gospel" at every High Mass, so I know it by heart. I held on to verse five in the weeks and months following September 11, 2001: "The light shines in the darkness, and the darkness has not overcome it." In the events of that day, the darkness engulfed all of us – yet the light still shines.

We saw courage, sacrifice, and heroism as never before. We experienced a new closeness with family and friends, and we became more aware of our need for each other. We recognized our dependence on God and came to terms with our own mortality. We saw the fragileness of life, and we learned to value the gifts that are ours. In all of this, the light still shines.

When I anticipate the unknown darkness that will overtake me in the new year, I remember that "the Light shines." When I fear that those I love will be hurt and I will stand helpless, I remember – "the Light shines." When I witness my own abilities slipping away, I remember – "the Light shines." When I consider the dark rooms of my inner self into which I must often go, I remember – "the Light shines."

We need not fear the darkness – because we know that the Light shines in the darkness, and the darkness will not overcome it!

~ Your Reflection ~

Leading Them Home   Matthew 18:12-14

What is your opinion? If a man has a hundred sheep and one of them goes astray, will he not leave the ninety-nine in the hills and go in search of the stray? And if he finds it, amen, I say to you, he rejoices more over it than over the ninety-nine that did not stray. In just the same way, it is not the will of your heavenly Father that one of these little ones be lost.

In the 1950's, there were still a lot of small, family-owned farms in rural Indiana. The farmers who were poor might have only one horse, cow, or pig – but no matter how poor the farmer was, he would never have only one sheep. Sheep are very social animals: an isolated sheep can quickly become bewildered and even neurotic. And if a sheep falls on its back, it can't get up by itself – left unaided, it will die. So, as kids on the farm, we knew that if a horse or cow got out of the pasture, it would sooner or later turn up nearby, or would find its own way back home. But if a sheep got out, there was a sense of urgency – because sheep will just aimlessly wander off and, if not found, will not survive.

So when we "wander off" in our lives, Jesus doesn't just lament the loss or assume that we'll sooner or later find our way "back home." There is a sense of urgency: the Good Shepherd goes searching for his lost sheep until it is found! The correlation of this passage from Matthew and the Advent readings from Isaiah is striking: we are in exile, a voice "crying out in the desert" – and Jesus the Shepherd is "crying out" for us, hoping that we will recognize his voice and return home.

When Winter Comes

Who is "in exile" and "crying out in the desert" today? Refugees from wars, the homeless on our streets, prisoners, orphans, the elderly in our nursing homes, to be sure. But there is more – all of us have times of "exile"; some have *lives* of "exile." And it isn't that we have purposely gone into "exile" – most often, we are like the sheep and have just "wandered away." We wander away from loved ones (we just don't make the effort to stay in touch anymore); we wander away from meaningful relationships (we just don't want to risk, or make the commitment); we wander away from the true purpose of our lives (we just want enough money and possessions to feel safe and secure); we wander away from our faith (we just don't have time for prayer or reflection). If we want to see a "lost sheep" or someone who is "in exile," all we need to do is look in the mirror!

To "come home" to God this Advent, we must become both the sheep and the shepherd. We must acknowledge our need for the help and love of others, and we must allow others to minister to us. We must also seek out the lost and the lonely, those who are "on their back" and need our help – those who have lost a loved one, those who are hungry or needy, and those who are alone. We must listen to those "voices crying in the desert" – the voices of those who are lost, and the voice of the One who wants us to be found.

In what ways have you "wandered off"? And who, in the words of Isaiah, are you "holding close to your heart and leading home?"

Cry Out in Your Desert   Isaiah 40:3, 6

A voice cries out:
In the desert prepare the way of the LORD!
    Make straight in the wasteland a highway for our God!
A voice says, "Cry out!"

"**W**hat do you want the most from the Advent and Christmas season?" This question was the focus of our prayer group's meeting. My friend's reply was almost inaudible: "I just want it to be over." She then shared her childhood experience of being locked in a closet for thirty days; her only human contact was when food was slid under the door. She explained that, as a result, she didn't feel joy and happiness at this time of year, and that societal expectations of those things only exacerbated her pain. Our eyes met, our hands touched; I wanted the holidays to be over too.

The summer was long and hot in the year that I got my first job: crawling across our neighbor's onion fields, pulling weeds with my siblings. He paid each of us the same rate as our age, so I was making seven cents an hour, and Mom had said it would be our Christmas money. Our neighbor said he couldn't pay us until the crop came in, but we didn't mind. The pages of our Sears catalog were smudged and worn from repeated reading, as we each dreamed of getting that special toy we always wanted. This year, Christmas would be different: it would be *good*. But, as summer turned into fall, the excuses began: the crop wasn't very successful, prices were down... besides, the kids hadn't worked all that hard.

When Winter Comes James R. Welter

Finally, Mom had to say the unthinkable – our neighbor would not be paying us for our summer's work. We would not be able to order anything from the Sears catalog; we would have to depend entirely on the charity of others for Christmas at our house this year. Again. When the time came, there was always the waiting: would anyone remember us this year? Would we have any gifts, any celebration at all? Some years were better than others; some years, no one came and Mom just did the best she could.

After the holidays, I dreaded going back to school. There would always be the inevitable chore of "sharing with the class what you got for Christmas." "Pants that no one had worn before" would only bring laughter, so I would lie again. And there was that big girl in the front row who knew I was lying; one year she would tell the whole class, and I would run from the room.

I just wanted it to be over.

For many people, this will be the first holiday season without a loved one. For others, it will be the third or the fourth or the tenth; the pain doesn't go away. Still others are alone this season, some in ways we can scarcely imagine: in prison, battling addiction, succumbing to illness, starving, abandoned, or living on the street. In all of this, Isaiah urges us to "Cry out!" (Is 40:6) He invites us to acknowledge our hurts, while offering us hope in the One who is to come.

Isaiah tells us it's OK to cry. It's OK to cry this Advent, this Christmas; it's OK to "cry out in your desert." To cry when that special song is sung; to cry as you hang that extra angel on the tree. To cry for a childhood denied. To cry for words never spoken; for songs never sung. To cry for Christmas as it was last year, or the year before, or ten years ago; to cry for the Christmases that will never be again.

Our hearts hold the pain, struggles, wonderings, yearnings, and desires that lie deep within. Isaiah is urging us to cry out to God in the sadness, grief, joys, hopes, and yearnings of our hearts. In these Advent weeks, Isaiah speaks of God's dwelling with us; he proclaims, "Comfort, give comfort to my people" (Is 40:1). He tells us that, if we hope in the Lord, we will "run and not grow weary, walk and not grow faint."(Is 40:31) He assures us that our Heavenly Father is always at our side, and tells us "like a shepherd he feeds his flock and gathers the lambs in his arms." (Is 40:11)

In saying all of this, Isaiah prepares us for the greatest message of all: "A young woman will bear a son and he shall be called Emmanuel – God is with us!"

Come, Lord Jesus!

When Winter Comes

James R. Welter

~ Your Reflection ~

The Tenth Chapter:
Death Into Life

It is the first Easter Sunday. Two disciples are on the road to Emmaus, which is "about seven miles from Jerusalem," and suddenly Jesus begins to walk with them. Scripture says, "They saw him but did not recognize him." Night is coming and it looks like Jesus will go on, but they invite him to stay. Break bread, share a meal, enter into a relationship with us... be a part of our lives. When the disciples extend that invitation, Jesus takes over. There is a reversal of roles, and Jesus breaks the bread. The stranger becomes a friend; the invited guest becomes the host. And in the sharing of a meal, in that intimate relationship – they recognize Jesus! Luke seems to say that to recognize Jesus, we must invite him in. And if we invite him in, he will take over our lives – and we will recognize him!

It is significant that Luke only names one of the disciples on that road – *we* are the other disciple! That is Luke's way of inviting *us* to enter the story, to walk the journey, to encounter Jesus. Each of us are on a different place in that journey: some have not yet met Jesus, while others have met Jesus, but do not recognize him in a personal way in their lives. Still others recognize Jesus, and are challenged to live out of that experience.

It is recognizing Jesus that brings us from death into life!

Stay in the Game   Matthew 1:18-19

Now this is how the birth of Jesus Christ came about. When his mother Mary was betrothed to Joseph, but before they lived together, she was found with child through the Holy Spirit. Joseph her husband, since he was a righteous man, yet un- willing to expose her to shame, decided to divorce her quietly.

Sometimes I wonder what those who choose the readings for the Lectionary are thinking when they make their selections. I mean, here we have a Christmas story that is usually read at Easter! In this "Christmas story at Easter," though, I'm hearing lessons of faith, trust, and perseverance. I'm hearing lessons of having the tenacity to just "stay in the game" – even if you're not sure exactly what the game is!

I think of Joseph as a pretty average, "salt-of-the-earth" kind of guy. He's "out of the loop." Others have visions, hear voices, and have stars guide them, but poor Joseph is always the last to know. He's just a "regular Joe" – he goes to work every day, tries to make a living, and does what he has to do. He stays focused on his family, and naturally wants to do what is best for them. So when he sees that his wife-to-be is already pregnant, he looks for a way to handle the situation in a manner that will be the least hurtful to her – he decides to "divorce her quietly." But when he is told that she is "with child through the Holy Spirit," he stays with her, despite his doubts. And when he learns in the middle of the night that his family is in danger, he gets up and takes them out of town without a second thought. In later years, when Joseph is journeying home with Mary and they find that the young Jesus is missing, Joseph simply turns around and goes back to find him. Although he never seems to know exactly what is going on with all of this, Joseph just tries to do what's right and "stays in the game."

Some of those traits were apparently passed to his son: Jesus, too, just naturally does what is right and, in times of doubt, uncertainty, and temptation, always elects to "stick with it," to "stay in the game." Sometimes that kind of determined tenacity – that stubbornness, that perseverance – is all that keeps *us* in the game, too!

When he knelt in the garden of Gethsemane, wanting with every fiber of his being for "this cup to pass," Jesus must have thought of his father (both of them!). Remember what your father taught you, he must have told himself… and trust in your heavenly Father! Just take a deep breath, grit your teeth, and do what's right…

… just stay in the game.

Not Far From The Kingdom   Mark 12:32-34

The scribe said to him, "Well said, teacher. You are right in saying, 'He is One and there is no other than he.' And 'to love him with all your heart, with all your understanding, with all your strength, and to love your neighbor as yourself' is worth more than all burnt offerings and sacrifices." And when Jesus saw that [he] answered with understanding, he said to him, "You are not far from the kingdom of God."

When we get the answer right in school, we expect a reward – a good grade, a prize, or at least recognition from the teacher… a "Good job!" or an "Atta boy/girl!"

The "student" in this passage, a scribe, answers the question right: love of God and love of neighbor fulfills the law. And Jesus tells him he is "not far" from the kingdom! "Wait a minute," he must have thought, "I got the answer right… I'm supposed to get a prize! What do you mean I'm 'not far'?? I thought I was right on!"

Well, no… you're close, but no cigar! Jesus uses this moment to teach the scribe and the crowd that love shows itself more strongly in actions than in words. You are "not far" because you have the words… but now you must show the actions. St. Francis understood that love must be reflected in actions when he said, "Preach the gospel every day… if all else fails, use words."

When Winter Comes

James R. Welter

In the season of Lent, we are reminded of the importance of actions. We are reminded of the importance of a love that cares for the sick and visits the imprisoned. We are reminded of the importance of a love that comforts the sorrowing, and sees Christ in the least of our sisters and brothers.

We, too, are "not far" from the Kingdom of God. We need only to act. To "put our money where our mouth is," to "walk the walk." To forgive, and be forgiven. To love, and be loved!

In what way will you "act out" your faith today?

~ Your Reflection ~

Betrayal   John 13:20-21

"Amen, amen, I say to you, whoever receives the one I send receives me, and whoever receives me receives the one who sent me."

When he had said this, Jesus was deeply troubled and testified, "Amen, amen, I say to you, one of you will betray me."

Why did Judas betray his Master?

Was his treachery motivated by greed? (It seems unlikely – thirty pieces of silver was a modest sum, in that time and place.) Did he feel bitter disappointment with Jesus? Or was it hatred, perhaps due to disillusionment?

It may be that Judas never intended for his Master to die. Certainly, Jesus had not acted to forcibly liberate the Jews from their hated Roman rulers, as many expected the Messiah to do. Perhaps Judas felt Jesus was proceeding too slowly, or not acting aggressively enough, in setting up the anticipated "messianic kingdom." Maybe Judas was trying to force the hand of Jesus, by setting up a confrontation that would *compel* the Messiah to act in the militant, dramatic manner Judas felt was necessary. If so, then the most basic sin of Judas was his refusal to accept Jesus for who he was – and his failure to trust that God has a plan and knows what's best.

How often we, too, try to "manipulate" God! We try to persuade him, to make deals with him, to control him –

to make him do our bidding. We want God to answer our prayers, to give us our miracle. And we want God to do it *our* way, in *our* time – in the manner *we* think he should do it! Because God just doesn't "do it right"! He doesn't obey! He doesn't act as *I* feel God should act! And I don't understand what he's doing. And so I fail to trust. I think I know better than God!

And in doing so, I too betray him.

God doesn't do it our way; God does it *God's* way. And we should not seek to bend God's ways to suit ourselves. Rather (as a line in the Jewish Talmud suggests), we should instead seek to bend *our* ways to suit God.

We cannot change God. Instead, we must allow God to change us.

In what ways will you allow God to change *you* today?

Good Friday   John 19:1-3

Then Pilate took Jesus and had him scourged. And the soldiers wove a crown out of thorns and placed it on his head, and clothed him in a purple cloak, and they came to him and said, "Hail, King of the Jews!" And they struck him repeatedly.

The cross brings us face-to-face with the suffering of Jesus. He was alone – his disciples had deserted him, except for his mother, three women, and John, the "beloved disciple." His death was humiliating – the public death of a common criminal – as well as agonizing. Normally, a crucified man could last for days on a cross; he usually died from exposure. But Jesus had already been scourged, beaten with rods, and had a crown of thorns pressed into his skull – little wonder that he died by mid-afternoon.

God comes face-to-face with what it means to be human today – with what it means to suffer.

For God is not merely *playing* at being human; the body of Jesus is not a disguise, nor a "second home." It's real – and it hurts. For the nails, God must open his hands – the hands that have sown the seeds. For the nails, God must lift his feet – the feet that have walked on the water. God is no longer hidden from our wants, from our fears. God is no longer remote in his heavenly shelter. God is one of us today. Alone. Abandoned. Stripped of everything.

When Winter Comes

James R. Welter

He is naked. He brought nothing with him into the world — none of our values, our goods, our profits, our selfish desires, our petty concerns... and he will take nothing from the world. He is going as naked as he came.

Jesus dies because the world didn't understand him: "They came looking for him with lanterns and weapons." Looking for the Light of the World with lanterns! Looking for the Prince of Peace with weapons!

In John's gospel, the first words of Jesus are: "What are you looking for?" And at the end of John's gospel, Jesus asks again: "Who are you looking for?"

He is asking you. He is asking me.

In teaching his catechism class, my brother asks his students: "Do you want to see Jesus? Do you want to see God? Then look at the person next to you. If you do not see him there... then you will never see him."

Do we look for Jesus where he is to be found? Do we look for Jesus where he said he would be? Or do we come looking for him with lanterns and weapons? Do we approach him with indifference? With contempt? With envy? With hate?

How will you look for Jesus in others today?

Amidst the Stones   Acts 7:58-60

*They threw him out of the city, and began to stone him.
The witnesses laid down their cloaks at the feet of a young
man named Saul. As they were stoning Stephen, he called
out, "Lord Jesus, receive my spirit." Then he fell to his knees
and cried out in a loud voice, "Lord, do not hold this sin
against them"; and when he said this, he fell asleep.*

Easter is my favorite holiday.

I like it because the major focus is a spiritual one: there is
none of the commercialism that is attached to Thanksgiv-
ing and Christmas. The joy of Easter reminds us that there
is hope. Hope that our lives have meaning. Hope that we
will see our loved ones again. Hope that death is not the
end. Hope that God loves us, comforts us, and will save us.

In celebrating Easter, however, it is easy to forget what
precedes that joy. It is easy to forget the dying.

In this passage, the story of Stephen (the first Christian
martyr) reminds us of the dying. The martyrs give
that greatest of gifts, their very lives – their very selves.
As Christians, we are asked to do the same. We are asked to
give our very selves! And we do, in our daily "dying" to
ourselves, in our letting go, and in our suffering.

In tough times, we want our miracle first. We want to skip
the dying! "Lord," we often pray, "make me well.
Spare this life. Return this child. Find me a job. Solve
this problem. Take this cup from me."

When Winter Comes

James R. Welter

When I pray, I usually include directions for God; I'm very good at telling God what to do! And if I were Stephen, my prayer would be clear: "Don't let them stone me!"

Stephen prays… but the stones still fall!

Stephen knows about the dying. He knows that the cup will not be taken away; even the Son was not spared. And "is the servant greater than the master?" So Stephen does not pray for that which God is not likely to give. And he does not pray only for himself. Instead, he prays for God's presence, God's comfort… and God's mercy upon his enemies.

God is not "testing" Stephen – *life* is testing Stephen! Those are real people throwing real stones. God does not *cause* these moments – although God is often *in* these moments. God does not stop the stones, but instead gives that which God always promises: strength, courage, wisdom, peace, comfort, forgiveness, hope… even joy!

So where are you, Jesus, when the stones are falling in my life?

"I am at your side, where I said I would be…

…standing with you, amidst the falling stones."

Sunday's Coming   Matthew 17:22-23

As they were gathering in Galilee, Jesus said to them, "The Son of Man is to be handed over to men, and they will kill him, and he will be raised on the third day." And they were overwhelmed with grief.

My office phone rang at 8:04 a.m. on the morning of my fifteenth anniversary with the company. I was the first person in the firm to reach that milestone and I moved quickly to the elevator, wondering what "surprise" gift had been selected to commemorate the occasion. Without even offering an invitation to sit down, my boss uttered the fateful words, "We're going to ask you to resign. Be out of here today, and have someone sign for your front-door key."

I was devastated. In shocked disbelief, I gathered my personal belongings from my office and put them in a box. There was the kindergarten footprint plaque from my son (bearing the inscription, "I love you with all my 'sole'"), my wife's picture, some family vacation photos, and my desk nameplate (a cherished gift from my staff).

And I left.

When I later called my brother for consolation, all he had to offer was a pithy little saying he had once heard from a Baptist preacher, who had ended a description of Jesus' suffering and death with the line: "But remember, it's only Friday – and Sunday's comin'!"

When Winter Comes

James R. Welter

In the following months, as I sought a new job, I heard over and over again: "You're too old." "You're over-quali-fied." "You're too expensive." And I found myself clinging to the words of that saying: "It's only Friday – and Sunday's comin'!" And when, after what seemed like an eternity, I finally got a new job, I called my brother and yelled into the phone, "IT'S SUNDAY!"

In this gospel passage, we hear one of at least three predictions that Jesus made to his followers about his coming death – his "Friday." The response of the disciples to the words of Jesus was grief; Matthew tells us that they were overwhelmed with grief. Mark and Luke also tell us that the disciples really didn't understand what Jesus was saying. They seem to have completely missed the point of the last words of Jesus on this occasion, "and he will be raised up on the third day." They missed the part about resurrection! They missed the fact that "Sunday's comin'!"

We know that, in this life, we will suffer. We are told that from Genesis to Revelation. We will experience all kinds of loss, pain, and hardship; we will have many "Fridays." But let's not forget the second part of our faith – that no matter what comes our way, no matter how bad things may get, or how terrible the suffering – that it's only Friday...

...and "Sunday's comin'!"

Do Not Cling To Me   John 20:15-17

Jesus said to her, "Woman, why are you weeping? Whom are you looking for?" She thought it was the gardener and said to him, "Sir, if you carried him away, tell me where you laid him, and I will take him." Jesus said to her, "Mary!" She turned and said to him in Hebrew, "Rabbouni," which means Teacher. Jesus said to her, "Stop holding on to me..."

"**I** come to the garden alone / while the dew is still on the roses / and He walks with me and He talks with me / and He tells me I am His own..."

I can still hear my mother humming that good old Baptist hymn as she worked around the house. A garden, for me, creates images of picking beans and killing bugs. The image of a garden is frequently found in scripture; it signifies a close personal relationship. It begins in the book of Genesis when God creates a garden and "comes down" and walks in the garden with Adam. It reflects the closeness of God to his creation and is a precursor to God "coming down" in human form to be one of us.

Every time we witness new life or observe a new season, we again become aware of the images in scripture of God as a gardener. We are reminded that we too have been planted, and are growing into death and life again. It is no wonder that Jesus spent his last night talking with his Father in a garden. And it is no surprise that Mary Magdalene encountered the risen Lord and mistook him or a gardener.

When Winter Comes

James R. Welter

Like that very first morning, God was sowing the seeds of surprise – the seeds of new life!

There was a classic commercial some years ago: the kids didn't want to try the new cereal, so they asked "Mikey" to do it. Throughout the gospels, the followers of Jesus want to use him as the easy way out, so they ask Jesus to do it: calm the storm, cure the sick, feed the multitudes. At times he gets exasperated: "Where is your faith?" "All this generation wants is a sign." "*You* feed them!"

In this gospel passage, Jesus tells Mary: "Stop holding on (clinging) to me…" Things have changed; I've got to go. When you cling, life is destroyed; when you hold on to anything, you cease to live. Let go of the illusion that I – or anyone else – can do it for you. "I have no hands but yours; I have no feet but yours." I cannot forgive you if you do not forgive others. I cannot heal those who do not believe. YOU have to do it: *you* feed them. *You* forgive them. *You* heal them. *You* visit them. *You* love them. *You* invite them to believe.

But Jesus – where will you be?

"I'll be where I always am: in the garden, walking with you."

Emmaus
Luke 24:13-16

Now that very day two of them were going to a village seven miles from Jerusalem called Emmaus, and they were conversing about all the things that had occurred. And it happened that while they were conversing and debating, Jesus himself drew near and walked with them, but their eyes were prevented from recognizing him.

It isn't surprising to find that one of the last stories in Luke's gospel is about a journey – Luke has used that writing style throughout his gospel and in the book of Acts.

It is the first Easter Sunday. Two disciples are on the road to Emmaus, which is "about seven miles from Jerusalem." Jesus is dead. He wasn't what they expected him to be, and now he's gone. Their hopes are dashed; they're hanging it up, calling it quits. They're heading home.

Suddenly, Jesus is walking with them on the road. Scripture says, "They saw him, but didn't recognize him."

Didn't recognize him?! Angels had told the women that Jesus was alive; the Easter message had been proclaimed. But the two disciples didn't recognize him! He recited scripture until their "hearts were burning" – but they didn't recognize him! He "interpreted every passage of scripture that pertained to him." He gave them all the "facts" – but they still didn't recognize him!

Then something happens that makes all the difference. Night is coming and it looks like Jesus is moving on.

When Winter Comes   James R. Welter

The two disciples could have said good-bye, like we do when we meet an interesting person on a bus or airplane: "It was nice meeting you; have a nice trip"… and it's over. Our life doesn't change. But instead, they say, "Stay with us." A richer translation says, "Abide with us" – break bread, share a meal, enter into a relationship with us. Be a part of our lives.

And when they extend that invitation, Jesus takes over. There is a reversal of roles, and Jesus breaks the bread. The stranger becomes a friend; the invited guest becomes the host. In the sharing of a meal, in that intimate relationship… they recognize him! Luke seems to be saying that, in order to recognize Jesus, we must invite him in. And if we invite him in, he will take over our lives – and we will recognize him!

It is significant that Luke only names one of the disciples on that road – *we* are the other disciple! It is Luke's way of inviting *us* into the story. He invites us to walk the journey, and to encounter Jesus.

Each one of us is at a different place on that journey. Some have not yet met Jesus, while others have met Jesus, but do not recognize him in a personal way in their lives. Still others recognize Jesus, and are challenged to live out of that experience.

To recognize Jesus, we must first invite him in.

How will you invite him into your life today?

The Eleventh Chapter:
September 11, 2001

Like each of you, I remember exactly where I was on September 11, 2001, when the United States was attacked by terrorists in New York City, Washington D.C., and Pennsylvania. I stood around a small television set in the parish office with my staff and we watched somberly as powerful symbols of our culture crumbled before our eyes.

Then there was the aftermath: "All airplanes are to land immediately and all flights are canceled." There was a sinking feeling in my stomach. My wife was overseas, maybe even in the air on the way home. I raced home to check her itinerary in a frantic attempt to determine her location. In one of those grace-filled moments, the phone rang five minutes after I arrived at the house: my wife was safe, but she was stranded in Rome and did not know when she would be able to return. For another eight agonizing days, I struggled to get airline information and waited anxiously for her e-mails.

I was not alone in my fear and anxiety. People came to church in great numbers in the days and weeks following the attacks, as we all experienced a new closeness with family and friends. We recognized our dependence on God and became more aware of our need for each other. We came to terms with our own mortality and saw the fragility of life.

215

The reflections in this section were the ones I shared in those uncertain days. I hope they remind us of that "winter" experience following the September 11th tragedy, when we remembered our God and turned to each other for strength.

Raise the Bar   Matthew 5:38-44

You have heard that it was said, "An eye for an eye and a tooth for a tooth." But I say to you, offer no resistance to one who is evil. When someone strikes you on [your] right cheek, turn the other one to him as well. If anyone wants to go to law with you over your tunic, hand him your cloak as well. Should anyone press you into service for one mile, go with him for two miles. Give to the one who asks of you, and do not turn your back on one who wants to borrow. You have heard that it was said,
"You shall love your neighbor and hate your enemy." But I say to you, love your enemies, and pray for those who persecute you.

Jesus raises the bar today. He quotes the old law: "…you shall give life for life, eye for eye, tooth for tooth, hand for hand, foot for foot, burn for burn, wound for wound, stripe for stripe" (Exodus 21:23-25). As cruel as this law may sound to us, it was an improvement over what was previously practiced. This law was meant to limit vengeance, so that, if someone steals your coat, you aren't justified in killing his family. In other words, the punishment must fit the crime. This law was not normally taken literally; it served as a guide for a judge when assessing punishment and penalty in a court of law (see Deuteronomy 19:18).

Jesus raises the bar today: he gives us a higher standard, not based on what is "fair" or legal, but based on grace and love. Jesus isn't actually giving a new law, nor is he doing away with the old law. Jesus is "fulfilling" the law – he's

217

redefining it. "Who is your neighbor?" he asks. Is your neighbor just the "sons of your own people"? Is your neighbor only those you care about, or live near, or associate with?

Jesus raises the bar today: our neighbor is *everyone*; there are no exceptions to love. We must not only avoid returning evil for evil, but we must seek the good of those who wish us ill. Jesus raises the bar today: we must "love our enemies."

There are no exceptions to love. Not when they slap your face. Not when they steal your cloak. Not when they crash airplanes into your buildings.

Jesus raises the bar today. Can we meet his standard?

Will we try?

Under the Ashes   Isaiah 25:7-8

On this mountain he will destroy
the veil that veils all peoples,
The web that is woven over all nations;
he will destroy death forever.
The Lord GOD will wipe away
the tears from all faces.

Anyone who has suffered a significant loss – whether it is the death of a loved one, a divorce, or any major misfortune – knows that the first year of grief is very difficult. All of those "first" events tend to intensify the pain. As a nation, this is our first holiday season – our first Advent – since the 9/11 tragedy. As a nation, we mourn. When the innocent were buried, our innocence was buried as well. We thought we were safe; we thought what we built would stand forever. Perhaps we should have known better. But we didn't.

When I read the words of Isaiah, I thought: it's as though a veil has been lifted and we now see things more clearly. Our illusions of security and safety are shattered, our innocence gone. We know now that our lives are not our own, that we are not in control. In *The Prophet*, Kahlil Gibran expresses that awareness when he speaks of children: "Your children are not your children. They come through you but not from you, and though they are with you yet they belong not to you…"

219

When Winter Comes James R. Welter

We do not "possess" life. It is not our own. It comes through us, but not from us. It is ours, but it does not truly belong to us.

Under the ashes, there is no race. Under the ashes, there are no differences. Under the ashes, life is known as the gift that it truly is.

The veil has been lifted.

Under the ashes, we are one!

~ Your Reflection ~

September 11, 2001

Fear and Praise   Luke 7:12-15

As he drew near to the gate of the city, a man who had died was being carried out, the only son of his mother, and she was a widow. A large crowd from the city was with her. When the Lord saw her, he was moved with pity for her and said to her, "Do not weep." He stepped forward and touched the coffin; at this the bearers halted, and he said, "Young man, I tell you, arise!" The dead man sat up and began to speak, and Jesus gave him to his mother.

The gentle approach of Jesus to the woman in this passage is touching. Of course he would be moved by compassion for her; we would feel compassion, too. And what wouldn't we give for the power to turn back the clock – to restore life? In this story, Jesus does just that – he restores life. "Then Jesus gave him back to his mother." It is a touching scene. But what is the first reaction of the mourners in the verse that follows? Fear!

Fear is our natural reaction in the presence of awesome power. Fear is our natural reaction, whether that power is good or evil. Fear – because we are in the presence of that which we cannot control and can sometimes barely comprehend. But notice their second reaction: "They began to praise God!" Fear – then praise.

I worked late the Friday night following the September 11th attacks. I didn't want to go home. My wife was still stranded in Europe and I knew the house would be empty. I thought of how our lives would change; we'll never fly again.

When Winter Comes

James R. Welter

Today, following 9/11, we stand in fear of the power of evil and destruction – power we cannot control or comprehend. A power that can paralyze us. A power that can destroy us. But hear the words of Jesus this day as he stands in the presence of evil and death: "I bid you, GET UP!" Don't let evil win. GET UP! Don't be afraid! It's time to praise God! Praise God, who will not let us be overcome by evil, but will give us strength. Praise God, who teaches us a better way. Praise God, because we know something that the evildoers do not – we know the power of the Resurrection. We know, as one Baptist preacher put it, that "Sunday's comin'!"

It's time to fly again!

The Long Haul　　　　　　　　Luke 9:1-3

He summoned the Twelve and gave them power and authority over all demons and to cure diseases, and he sent them to proclaim the kingdom of God and to heal [the sick]. He said to them, "Take nothing for the journey, neither walking stick, nor sack, nor food, nor money, and let no one take a second tunic."

We have heard it so many times since 9/11: "We're in this thing for the long haul." There are no easy answers; there is no "quick fix." We must seek justice. We must protect the innocent. Do we have the stamina? Do we have the resolve?

After a period of preaching, teaching, and healing in Galilee, Jesus now commissions and instructs the Twelve to go and do likewise. He gives them their marching orders: they are to take no staff or traveling bag, no bread or money, only one coat, and they are to accept others' hospitality. Why does Jesus tell the apostles to "travel light," carrying so few provisions?

The "light load" we are to carry, this "poverty of spirit" we are to embrace, frees us from greed and any preoccupation with material possessions. It builds faith and allows God to provide. The Lord wants his disciples to rely on him. These are stark directives for a specific journey: "Go out and try this and report back." It's for the "short haul."

When Winter Comes

James R. Welter

Jesus also commissions and instructs *us*, but our journey involves the "long haul." There are no easy answers, no "quick fix." This long haul may require some prioritizing of our values and some adjustments to our lifestyle.

My wife is a hospice nurse; she deals with death every day. To help me keep my priorities straight, she will often remind me that she has never experienced anyone saying, at the end of their life: "I wish I had spent more time at the office!" I noticed that, on 9/11, not one of those last phone calls from the doomed airliners or buildings was a call to check on the stock market, or to see if a business deal got closed!

We are commissioned by this gospel passage to preach, to teach, and to heal — and we are in it for the "long haul." We preach through the example of our lives. We teach by sharing our faith experiences with others. We heal by being present to each other in times of distress and need. Often it's not a very dramatic journey, and sometimes the way isn't clear to us. We don't have the certainty of a thunderbolt knocking us from our horse, or the assurance of a burning bush! Our call is simply to respond in love to the needs of the moment. To respond, to respond, to respond — until Jesus calls us home!

In the words of our President: "Do we have the stamina? Do we have the resolve?"

Sitting In God's Lap Matthew 18:2-3

He called a child over, placed it in their midst, and said, "Amen, I say to you, unless you turn and become like children, you will not enter the kingdom of heaven."

We saw it in the aftermath of 9/11; we sensed it, we felt it – the need to be together. I didn't want to go home to an empty house during that first week after the attacks. At the parish, we saw record numbers of people at Mass – and afterwards, they just "hung around" in our gathering space. In times of national or personal crisis, we need someone to be with us. We need to be in the presence of others.

Disasters such as the one that befell us as a nation on 9/11 require the presence of others to help us cope with the fear and pain. There is nothing more sacred in the context of human suffering than presence – than "just being there." We often feel awkward in the presence of suffering, pain, and death: we want to do something, but often there is nothing we can do. We want say something, but usually there is nothing we can say.

God knows our need for presence. The prophet Zechariah, for example, shows us an astounding vision of unity among the peoples of many cities and nations, who all seek to join the people of Israel because they have heard that God is present among them. God's name was revealed to Moses as "the One Who Is," or "the One Who Is Present." Jesus is called "Emmanuel," which means "God is with us."

225

When Winter Comes
James R. Welter

Presence is God's greatest gift. God does not abandon us in our suffering – he is Emmanuel; he is the "One Who Is Present." God is suffering with us right now! We may wonder how God can suffer – isn't he happy in Heaven? I can't answer that question directly, given the unknowable nature of God. But I can answer it in the context of what we know about love: when we love someone and they suffer, we "feel" their pain as well. So God – who *is* Love – must, by that very fact, somehow feel our pain. Thus, God suffers with us.

Jesus taught us to come to God as little children – innocent, trusting, needing and relying on God's love, care, and presence. I have often read this passage and thought of the "least" among us as the "children": the sick, the poor, the despised, the ones who are suffering or dying. But today I stand in their number, for I too am powerless. I too am helpless; I too am afraid.

Children (before we teach them otherwise) have no need to be the best, the first, or the greatest. They are content to simply "sit in God's lap." In the aftermath of that terrible, devastating day, we, too, need to become as little children. We need to recognize our powerlessness. We need to acknowledge our helplessness. We need to know that our God is with us. And like children, we need to be content. We need to be still…

…and simply sit in God's lap.

Don't Just Look Busy   Luke 12:47-48

That servant who knew his master's will but did not make preparations nor act in accord with his will shall be beaten severely; and the servant who was ignorant of his master's will but acted in a way deserving of a severe beating shall be beaten only lightly. Much will be required of the person entrusted with much, and still more will be demanded of the person entrusted with more.

My wife loves to shop. And there must be a lot of men like me who tire of shopping pretty quickly, because there is usually a chair provided for the "faint of heart"! Sometimes I pass time in that chair by looking at nearby signs. A favorite one I've seen says: "Jesus is coming – look busy!"

There was a time that I found the passage that says "to those who have been given much, much will be expected" to be a burdensome one. I saw it as adding more pressure, more expectations, more "shoulds" and "oughts." After all, arriving at an early hour in the vineyard has its responsibilities; the day will be long before the Master returns. (As kids, we used to say that the good thief dying on the cross next to Jesus was "lucky," because he didn't have to work too hard – he slipped into heaven at the last minute!)

Coming early does have its responsibilities: we have a long day ahead, and the Lord expects us to make good use of the gifts and graces he gives to us. And the more he gives, the more he requires of us. This passage reminds us not to be lazy and "take it easy" while the Master is away. Nor can we rely on just "looking busy" when he returns! We must get to work; we are not to put off until tomorrow what we know the Master expects us to do today!

And what are those "gifts" we have been given? What are the things that obligate us to "give much"? Our gifts and talents? Yes. Our financial resources? Absolutely. But there is more! The Lord himself is our gift and our treasure, and it is that gift that we are most expected to share! God calls us early into the fields, to work in his vineyard. He offers us a relationship with him and promises us eternal life. It is a duty, a privilege, and a joy to be called — but we dare not be idle. We must do the work, we must share the gifts; we must "tell the others."

The tragedy of September 11th reminds us that tomorrow is always uncertain, and that there's no time to waste.

Jesus is coming… let's *get* busy!

No Outsiders   Acts 10:9-16

The next day, while they were on their way and nearing the city, Peter went up to the roof terrace to pray at about noontime. He was hungry and wished to eat, and while they were making preparations he fell into a trance. He saw heaven opened and something resembling a large sheet coming down, lowered to the ground by its four corners. In it were all the earth's four-legged animals and reptiles and the birds of the sky. A voice said to him, "Get up, Peter. Slaughter and eat." But Peter said, "Certainly not, sir. For never have I eaten anything profane and unclean." The voice spoke to him again, a second time, "What God has made clean, you are not to call profane." This happened three times, and then the object was taken up into the sky.

We sometimes idealize the early Church. Scripture records witnesses remarking, "See how these Christians love each other!" The book of Acts also records that "many sold what they had and put it at the feet of the Apostles to be shared with the community" (Acts 1:45-47). Given the current scandals in the Church today, we may long for those "good old days."

But this passage from Acts reminds us that controversy and struggles in the Church are nothing new. Jesus was hardly out of sight when arguments started about who should be included in the new community. Was the good news only for the "chosen people"? How were "outsiders" to be dealt with? Was it necessary that newcomers obey the traditional Jewish dietary laws?

229

When Winter Comes
James R. Welter

One day, Peter has a dream. For the first time – for one brief, shining moment – he understands what Jesus meant! Everyone is included in God's kingdom and "there shall be one flock, one shepherd." It was so clear in that dream! But it's morning now, and Peter is challenged by the "circumcised believers." He must have misunderstood the dream: *everyone* included? That can't be right! We shout, too: but that makes "them" the same as "us"! You mean God's kingdom includes the person at work who backstabs and sabotages me at every turn? The anger-addicted bully who holds a position of power? The annoying, argumentative neighbor? The petty, grudge-holding relative? The vindictive "ex"? (That wasn't a dream, Pete; that was a nightmare!) The non-Catholic? (Come on now!) The non-Christian? (You've got to be kidding!) It certainly can't include the prostitutes and sinners! You've got to draw the line! How about the immoral and greedy CEO? Draw the line. The child abuser? Draw the line. The convicted killer? This is getting out of hand! Draw the line. The 9/11 terrorists? Draw the line. Osama bin Laden? Draw the line. Saddam Hussein? Draw the line.

Luckily for us, we don't have to draw the line, nor should we – God does that. The amazing thing is that God's line seems to be a circle! A circle – and we're *all* inside. As far as the Good Shepherd is concerned, there are no outsiders. He would die for each and every one of us. He would die for Osama bin Laden. He would die for Saddam Hussein.

He would die for me!

For This I Bless You Most   Matthew 25:33-37

He will place the sheep on his right and the goats on his left. Then the king will say to those on his right, "Come, you who are blessed by my Father. Inherit the kingdom prepared for you from the foundation of the world. For I was hungry and you gave me food, I was thirsty and you gave me drink, a stranger and you welcomed me, naked and you clothed me, ill and you cared for me, in prison and you visited me." Then the righteous will answer him and say, "Lord, when did we see you hungry and feed you, or thirsty and give you drink?"

By definition, parables have a surprise ending. We get what we do not expect, and we have to ask ourselves why. It is certainly no surprise when the "bad guys" – those who failed to feed the hungry or clothe the naked – plead: "But Lord, when did we see you hungry?" They don't understand. They don't "get it." And of course, they have an excuse – they didn't *see* the Lord hungry in the least of their brothers and sisters.

But it's interesting that when the "good guys" get welcomed into Paradise – they ask exactly the same question! "But Lord, when did we see you hungry?" They don't seem to "get it" either! They don't understand! Why not? Didn't they realize what they were doing?

We can take the answer from our own newspaper headlines about September 11, 2001. The reply of the "good guys" in this scripture passage calls to mind the slightly confused responses given by many of the police officers and

231

firefighters who answered the call of duty on 9/11. When asked by reporters how they were able to run into the burning twin towers and risk their lives to help others, many responded by saying something like: "Well, somebody had to do it... I was just doing my job..." The lack of pride or arrogant self-assurance in their responses reminds us that these people don't see themselves as heroes – they truly are ordinary people "just doing their job." It also tells us that doing the right thing is second nature to them – so second nature that they don't think of doing the right thing as something out of the ordinary.

So, in the words of the parable, they "fed the Lord when he was hungry" without knowing it. And why didn't they know it? Because they feed *anyone* who's hungry – that's just what they do. That *is* "their job." And it should be ours, too.

"When did we see you hungry, Lord, and feed you?" Was it when we gave a dollar to that beggar on the street, rather just pass him by? Was it when we went out of our way to help someone we didn't like, simply because he or she needed help and we happened to be there? Was it when we put aside an old grudge to comfort an estranged friend or relative? Or perhaps when we gave the benefit of the doubt to someone who may not have deserved it? Was it when we took a deep breath and did the right thing, just because it was right?

Yes, says the Lord. Anytime you were good, kind, compassionate, or loving toward others. That's when it was.

"But," we say, "that's nothing special! We do that sort of thing all the time!"

And God says: "Yes, I know. That's the point."

In the words of Kahlil Gibran: "For this I bless you most, you gave – and knew not that you gave at all."

To whom will you give of yourself today?

James R. Welter II

~ Your Reflection ~

When Winter Comes

James R. Welter

~ Your Reflection ~

The Twelfth Chapter

Just as the prophets of old were sent "to comfort the afflicted and to afflict the comfortable," so it is with God's Word.

God's Word is meant to assure us of his love and care during our times of stress and need... and it is also meant to challenge us in our "good times." We are continually challenged to "go and do likewise," and live out the message we have heard – to feed the hungry, to clothe the naked; to love God and love our neighbor. We are challenged to become that which we eat at the Lord's Table: bread broken and wine poured out. We are challenged to become one of the disciples, to be the ongoing presence of Jesus in our world.

I have not written anything for the Twelfth Chapter. This final chapter is the one that *you* write!

Throughout this book, space has been provided for your notes and personal observations. How has your image of God changed as you spent time with these scripture reflections? What new insights have you gained into your relationship with Jesus? In what ways have these reflections aided your self-knowledge and personal growth?

(continued)

When Winter Comes James R. Welter

I hope you have found these reflections both a comfort and a challenge. In a sense, this final chapter is not the end, but the beginning. Throughout this book, many of the reflections have concluded by asking "what will *you* do?" So what will you do now, to put your new insights and knowledge into action? What will you do now, to follow Jesus more closely as you live out your faith?

What will you do now, to "write" your Twelfth Chapter?

~ Your Reflection ~

INDEX
By Reflection Title

INDEX
By Bible Chapter & Verse

OLD TESTAMENT

NEW TESTAMENT

You may order additional copies of

When Winter Comes

Via our website, **www.AscendingView.com**

OR

Send check or money order for $13.95 per copy,
plus $2.50 shipping and handling
(Indiana residents add 6% sales tax) to:

**Ascending View Publications
231 Crosby Drive
Indianapolis, IN 46227**

Please include your name, address and telephone
number with your order.

Volume discounts available on quantities
of 20 or more.